THE LAWS OF SUCCESSFUL
SELLING

Fresh ideas to close that deal!

Alfred Tack

VERMILION
LONDON

1 3 5 7 9 10 8 6 4 2

Copyright © 1975 by Alfred Tack

The right of the late Alfred Tack, under the auspices of TACK Training
International, has been upheld under the Copyright, Designs
and Patents Act, 1988, to be identified as the author of this work.

Extracts from HOW TO TRAIN YOURSELF TO SUCCEED IN SELLING
and HOW TO INCREASE YOUR SALES TO INDUSTRY
have been revised and included in this book.

First published in the United Kingdom by Cedar,
an imprint of Mandarin Paperbacks.
This edition published in the United Kingdom in 2000 by
Vermilion, an imprint of Ebury Press,
Random House, 20 Vauxhall Bridge Road, London SW1V 2SA.

Random House Australia (Pty) Limited
20 Alfred Street, Milsons Point, Sydney,
New South Wales 2061, Australia

Random House New Zealand Limited
18 Poland Road, Glenfield,
Auckland 10, New Zealand

Random House South Africa (Pty) Limited
Endulini, 5a Jubilee Road, Parktown 2193, South Africa

Random House UK Limited Reg. No. 954009

www.randomhouse.co.uk

A CIP catalogue record for this book is available from the British Library

ISBN 0 09 185 606X

Typeset in Baskerville by MATS, Southend-on-Sea, Essex
Printed and bound in Denmark by Nørhaven, Viborg

Papers used by Vermilion are natural, recyclable products
made from wood grown in sustainable forests.

Contents

Editor's Comment:

Throughout this text, we use the generic terms 'seller', 'sales-person', etc., and 'buyer' for communication convenience.

In business today, a 'seller' is very often not someone who has the word 'sales' in their job title, but could be a director, a technical advisor or a customer service representative. Similarly, buyers are not necessarily people from purchasing departments. They may be company chairmen, chief accountants, office managers or personal assistants. Readers are asked to be very flexible in their interpretation of these terms.

Furthermore, although this book has been revised, its general assumption of the masculine gender for both buyers and sellers emphasises how much the workplace has changed since it was first written.

TACK TRAINING

Alfred Tack was the founder of the world-renowned training consultancy which bears his name. Tack courses are run in over 40 countries and 25 languages, and cover communication, finance, management, marketing and sales topics like the one in this book.

For information, contact:

TACK TRAINING INTERNATIONAL
[+44] (1494) 766611
Website: www.tack.co.uk

I

The Selling Personality

Have you the right kind of personality for salesmanship? Before you can answer this question you must examine another – what is the right kind of selling personality?

Some people can only define a sales personality as a seller who is over-selling. To them, someone with the 'gift of the gab' is a sales agent. The next stage in this train of thought is that *a selling personality means a salesperson who is a fast talker*. This is sheer nonsense. Yet the expression *He talks like a salesman* is often used.

Under the section devoted to personality in the *Encyclopedia Britannica*, the opening paragraph begins:

> Personality is the characteristic way of thinking and acting which identifies each person as a unique individual. Since it is the one psychological concept which impresses all the functions of the individual, it has become the basic integrating concept of psychology. Each theory or school of psychology gives a different approach to personality, yet all agree in placing it as a keystone in the arch of mental science.

We can read many books, study authorities, listen to words of wisdom from lecturers in psychology – and we still find a definition of personality elusive. Yet, strange as it may seem, we all know what personality means, without being able to define it. When we refer to a clash of personalities between two people we know why they cannot have a friendly relationship. When we are told that someone has a grim personality, again we know exactly what is meant.

Our customers understand as little about personality as we do, but they also know what they mean when they describe a salesperson as having a likeable personality. A sales personality, then, is one that builds friendship and understanding with the greatest number of prospective buyers or customers. It must:

> gain the confidence of a buyer
> win the respect of a buyer
> win the friendship of a buyer
> indicate to the buyer that he cannot be browbeaten.

But a salesperson's personality must not:

> leave an untrustworthy impression
> antagonise the buyer
> be so weak that a customer knows he can dominate the salesperson.

Good buyers should not be swayed by personal preferences, but they do, to a greater or lesser extent when all things are equal, favour those salespeople with whom they have a friendly relationship. It often happens – especially when selling to retail stores – that a seller calls repeatedly and rarely sees a buyer. The cause of this might well be that the seller has antagonised the assistant, who does not even bother to take his card; or that the buyer himself has little respect for the salesperson. It would be very salutary if salespeople could overhear the remarks of buyers when an assistant hands them a visiting card:

> 'Oh, not *him* again. Do get rid of him.'
> 'That bore? No, I won't see him – he just wastes my time.'
> 'I can't be bothered with him – tell him I'm busy.'

But every salesperson believes that such remarks always refer to the other fellow.
The psychologist William James said:

> *The greatest discovery of my generation is that human beings can alter their lives by altering their attitude of mind.*

How can the mind of a seller be changed so that it is reflected in his personality? Quite easily – by developing the right mental attitude and studying human relations.

Successful salespeople must have four personalities that combine into one. They must have a cheerful personality, a strong personality, a kindly personality, and a sincere personality. Linked together, they form the *selling* personality.

A CHEERFUL PERSONALITY

Nobody likes the company of miserable or depressing people – least of all buyers. Most of us have troubles enough of our own without being forced to listen to the ills and misfortunes of comparative strangers. Even members of a family do not take kindly to listening to near relatives describing in detail their operations, or lecturing on the decadence of modern society.

Too many people are depressing. Why should a seller expect a customer to be absorbed by the illnesses of himself or his family, the gruesome accident just witnessed, the depth of snow outside his house, the rapid spread of an influenza epidemic, his fibrositis or rheumatism, or his migraine headaches, his children's complaints or his problems with relatives? The list is lengthy. Of course, some gloomy people relish sadness and misfortune so that they, in their turn, can elaborate on their own complaints. Most of us, however, prefer cheerfulness to dejection, laughter to tears.

Never, then, for the rest of your selling life, tell a depressing story or give a despondent view of the world to customers. If a customer starts to depress you with his stories, listen but do not retaliate. The first stage in developing a happy and cheerful personality is to renounce boring others with your troubles. No matter how tempting it is to say, 'I have a splitting headache,' or 'I've a shocking cold,' resist it. And no one, but no one, is ever interested in whatever operation you may have undergone.

Being described as a cheerful person is a very good accolade to win for yourself.

A STRONG PERSONALITY

Strength comes to a salesperson from confidence and knowledge. A buyer meeting a salesperson who is unsure of herself will weaken her still more. Some instinct informs the buyer which salespeople he can push around and which he must respect. Years of dealing with a particular salesperson may condition the regard a customer has for her. The buyer will have learned how to handle her, just as a good seller will know how to deal with every type of buyer. The weak salesperson will, however, have shown her insufficiency on many occasions by her colourless personality and her readiness to accept unfair demands (such as special discounts and deliveries). Buyers take advantage of a weak salesperson. For the weak person to change in mid-career is difficult. If she has won a reputation for softness and timidity, no sudden change will alter it. And any change will probably take a long time. She can, however, ensure that she gives a stronger impression to *new* customers.

The young salesperson making her way in the world can easily develop a strong personality. She needs thorough product knowledge and must refuse to accede to the unfair whims of buyers. This will not lose her many orders. She must not show weakness by criticising her company or its products. To her, it must always be: my company – *right or wrong*.

A buyer forms an impression of a seller during the first few seconds of the approach, and will retain it as long as the relationship lasts. Your prospect will judge you by:

Your appearance. Even in these free and easy days, smartness is still a sign of a good business person, and buyers respect good business people.

The way you walk. Never slouch: it suggests a *couldn't-care-less* attitude. If the seller doesn't care about his products, why should a buyer be interested in them? The brush-off is easily given to the sloucher. Never hesitate. The hesitator walks a few steps, stops indecisively, continues for a few more steps, stops again to inspect something or look around . . . he looks like someone trying to keep up his courage.

The strong seller never slouches, hesitates or seems arrogant. He holds his shoulders back and walks briskly towards the buyer as though he is not only delighted to see him, but is certain he can do him a good turn. The buyer can judge the strength of a seller by the way he approaches.

The handshake. Don't shake hands with someone you have not previously met unless that person offers to shake hands with you. Some prospects dislike shaking hands with every salesperson who calls upon them. If you do shake hands, however, do so in a proper manner. Don't show off by trying to wrench the prospect's arm from its socket. Don't be too friendly, clasping him by the arm with one hand as you shake hands with the other. Don't shake his hand as if you were working a pump – he doesn't want his arm to be jerked rapidly up and down. Don't give him a *flannel* handshake. You know what a limp flannel feels like – that sort of handshake takes all the enthusiasm out of your approach. Don't shake hands at all if your hands are clammy. Don't try to wipe them with your handkerchief as you walk towards your prospect.

Clasp the prospect's hand firmly, give ONE SHAKE, and leave it at that.

Enthusiasm

The weak sales agent is rarely an enthusiast. Most strong people have tremendous enthusiasm for their work and they are not afraid to show it. Only one thing is more infectious than enthusiasm, and that is the lack of it. The buyer who hesitates about placing an order wants his mind made up for him, and the enthusiast can do that.

This is how enthusiasm has been defined:

> *Fire in the belly* was how the Greeks described that most infectious of all human emotions – enthusiasm.

> Everyone is an enthusiast about something – whether it is children, gardens, cars, windsurfing, etc. Someone may not be excitable, but note the light in his eyes and the interest in his voice when he talks about his loves.

> Many jobs can be carried out successfully without involving the emotions, but selling is not one of them. A seller is paid not only to communicate an idea, but also to stimulate possible buyers to act upon it. It is not enough for the salesperson to prepare a beautifully balanced sales

presentation. Life and conviction must be breathed into it before it can be expected to make an impact. I have known people with a great gift for logical thinking, and blessed with an extensive vocabulary, who have failed utterly as salespeople simply because they lacked the enthusiasm necessary to convince the buyer.

We British, once renowned for preserving a stiff upper lip under all conditions, are sometimes too determined to bend over backwards in an attempt to appear unbiased. This gives rise to the sort of wishy-washy sentence used on me recently by a visiting sales agent: 'I think, sir, that if perhaps you go in for this little piece of equipment you might find, as others have done, that it will do a fairly good job for you.' What sort of conviction is conveyed by such a statement? It is so loaded with half-doubts that it almost constitutes the warning: *Buy at your peril.*

Today we read a lot about people who are *uncommitted*. A seller can never be a member of this fraternity. He is committed, heart and soul, to his company and its products or services.

If he cannot find it in himself to be this way, then it is my belief that he should seek a company and a product to which he will wholly commit himself, and on whose behalf he will sell with enthusiasm. If he is not prepared to invest this quality in his selling, no matter what the company or product, then he should turn his attention to another type of work, less demanding in its need for self-investment.

Before he takes this final step, though, he should at least appreciate how other salespeople develop an enthusiasm for selling. They study their product or service back-to-front and inside-out. They find out all they can about their competitors. They become experts on their subject. Their work takes on some of the interest and appeal of a hobby – they become enthusiasts.

Now don't misunderstand – I am not suggesting that you should work yourself into a lather of simulated excitement in front of the customer. Enthusiasm is not an act; it is the manifest confirmation of sincerely held beliefs. If you are a quiet person, then your enthusiasm must be expressed accordingly, but it must be expressed. Enthusiasm in selling is judged not by how loudly a person shouts, but by how convincingly he talks. A seller without enthusiasm is like a bell without a clapper. He may look the part, but he will never sound it.

To develop a strong personality, be an enthusiast.

Admit Your Mistakes

The weak person is reluctant to admit that she has made a mistake, and will never apologise when proved to be wrong. She prefers to try and justify her error.

The person who believes that she never makes mistakes cannot be helped. Strangely, she is always the first to say, 'When I am wrong I will be the first to admit it.' Unfortunately, she never thinks she *is* wrong. Anyone who learns to admit mistakes can give herself a happier life and improve her salesmanship.

It is sometimes very difficult to say 'I'm sorry', but the effects of these two words can be great. Many people say they are sorry, but never sound as if they mean it, the implication being that they are taking the blame although the mistake was not theirs.

You will build an inner strength if, before justifying yourself, you pause to consider whether you are really right, or whether you are trying to disguise a mistake. During the pause, if you feel that you are in the wrong, smile and say, 'I'm sorry, it was my fault.'

Don't Boast

Because most people want to feel important, even the strong person may talk of his successes to create a good impression. The weak person, however, often boasts when he has nothing to brag about, and so develops the wrong type of personality. He may close an easy sale, but in his account of it to friends, everything is dramatised. He enters a dream world. This may inflate his own ego, but it only lessens the regard of others. The timid boy who would run fast if a girl made advances to him boasts of his conquests. The seller who is afraid of a buyer will describe how he cut that buyer down to size. Another salesperson, scared of the manager above him, will tell his wife how he put him in his place. No one likes to listen to the boasting of others. Weak people never learn that the more they brag, the weaker they seem to their fellow men.

Ask Advice

How do you react when someone asks your advice? You may have been consulted about something you know about or can do well. Doesn't it give you a rather warm glow – a feeling of well-being and self-importance? This is quite normal.

If most people are pleased to give advice, why is their help not sought more often? Too many take it as a sign of weakness to seek advice. They would rather be labelled as know-alls.

But it is strength, not weakness, to ask the advice of someone competent to give it.

The tycoons of industry would not make a decision without conferring with eminent lawyers, accountants, financiers, scientists, or doctors. That is a sign of their strength. Many a small trader relies on his own judgment and then complains of his bad luck. A seller should never be reluctant to ask the advice of a customer on any aspects of marketing and trading – on buying trends in a district, on buyers' views on packaging, on changes in the locality, on display. A buyer will warm to a salesperson who genuinely needs his advice. You always gain strength by having the courage to ask for advice from others.

Criticism

Laurence Sterne wrote in *Tristram Shandy:*

> *Of all the cants which are canted in this canting world – though the cant of hypocrites may be the worst – the cant of criticism is the most tormenting.*

This sums up the evils of criticism. Those who criticise while pretending to be helpful are often giving vent to spite. There are exceptions – unimaginative people with closed minds who believe in their divine right to criticise others, and that their caustic remarks are welcomed.

But no one likes his critics. Those paid to criticise plays or novels are not thanked by their victims. No statue has been erected to the memory of a critic. Few dramatic or literary critics are objective. They betray their own frustrations, lacking the creative impulse themselves; but their writings entertain. They dip their pens in vitriol and no one need read their criticisms if he doesn't want to. But paid critics are only a tiny minority of the population. It is we, the unpaid ones, who can do so much harm to others – as well as to ourselves – by our criticism.

A man meets a friend who has purchased a new sports car. This is how he greets him: 'But whatever made you buy it? If I'd known, I certainly would have stopped you from making this mistake. You should have bought a Ferrari – it's a far better car. Do you know the brand of car you bought had a lot of brake trouble last year? I would get it checked if I were you. A friend of mine had one and it broke down in the middle of nowhere because the automatic steering gave out. And another thing . . .'

Unnecessary criticism never profits anyone. A purchase has been made – perhaps of a car or a CD player or a set of golf clubs. The owner has paid money and is satisfied with the expenditure. What good can it do to make him regret that he bought X instead of Y? He cannot change it; he will have to live with it, so why not leave him feeling happy with his lawn mower or new television?

If we cannot help other people, then we should not harm them. Dissatisfaction with a purchase can cause misery. Make it a rule, therefore, never to criticise for the sake of criticism. Remember also that, when a friend invites you to criticise, he doesn't really want it – he is asking for your praise.

When you ask someone:

'What do you think of this mountain bike?'
'What do you think of my roses?'
'What do you think of this photo I took in the South of France?'

Do you want these answers:

'That's about the worst bike on the market.'

'You must have pruned badly – they are much too small.'

'Why don't you learn to take a decent picture, and stop kidding yourself that you're a first-class amateur photographer?'

Or do you want these answers:

'A very good bike, that.'

'A lovely rose.'

'That's a great photo – let me look at it again.'

Judge for Yourself

There are times when you must criticise – occasions when it is essential to explain carefully that a mistake is being made or that disaster looms ahead if a course of action is not altered. But before pointing this out, you must be convinced that there is no alternative.

Remember, then, to criticise only if it is essential; and if you must criticise, ensure that your opinion is presented in an acceptable manner.

A strong personality is built upon a determination to win respect by acting towards others as you would have them act towards you.

A FRIENDLY PERSONALITY

You can check whether you have a friendly personality. How do your buyers' subordinates react to your visits? A shop assistant, a worker at a bench, a supervisor or a personal assistant can undo all the good work that a salesperson has put in with a buyer. The seller without awareness and a friendly personality may wonder why he misses so many orders. An order has been promised – it has only to be countersigned and posted – but it doesn't come, and the seller wonders why. It often happens that some assistant has changed the buyer's mind.

The salesperson who puts on an act of friendship may deceive a buyer and his assistant for a time, but like all acts, it will be seen through in the end. Assistants in all businesses know instinctively which salespeople have friendly personalities and which are only making a pretence of friendship. If a seller is met with cordiality by everyone, from the receptionist to the managing director, then he has a friendly personality. And it is not acquired by sycophancy or flattery.

A friendly personality does not include switching on the charm, or being ingratiating. It is a personality that radiates warmth and friendship. A dictionary definition of friendliness is *attachment from mutual esteem*. When the seller wins the esteem and friendship of the buyer, selling becomes so much easier.

Don't Be Funny

You don't win friends by being known as a funny man. Except maybe after a few drinks in a pub, few people appreciate a string of funny stories. One is enough. Others in the gathering are too intent on telling their own favourite anecdotes.

Very few top business executives tell story after story. It is the lesser ones, eager to attract attention to themselves, who begin: 'Have you heard this one . . .' It is their only chance, for a few fleeting seconds, to capture the limelight. The more stories a person tells, the more boring he becomes.

Television presents the cream of the world's comedians – people who devote their lives to making others laugh and have highly paid script writers to feed them with matter and patter. Even so, seven out of ten of their stories fall flat. Some hardly raise a ripple of laughter. Yet many people – especially sales staff – consider they are good at telling funny stories. They have only to remember how they feel about the stories told to them to appreciate how theirs are received.

Take no notice of the laughter after one of your stories – it is often forced and unreal. Only the exceptional story, told by the exceptional storyteller, is worth hearing.

You do not develop a friendly personality by telling funny stories. Listen attentively to others, but refuse to retaliate.

Remember Names

We all love the person who remembers our name. We dislike anyone who mispronounces our name, and we have little regard for those who call us Mr Er . . . or Mr Um . . .

Frank Case said, *I think it humanly impossible for anyone to think of his own name as a word of little importance.* But many sellers do not bother to find out he names of prospective buyers before calling. How proud the average person feels when a head waiter greets him by name. The customer preens himself when, after one visit to a shop, the assistant remembers his name. A buyer reacts in the same way.

Here is an approach that a salesperson might make:

> 'Good morning, Mrs Johnson, it is good of you to spare me your time. This is how we can cut down waste, Mrs. Johnson – just look at this . . .'

Read that aloud. Read it again, but leave out Mrs Johnson's name. It doesn't sound the same, does it?

For a friendly personality you must always remember the other person's name – the names of shop assistants, mechanics, personal assistants and, of course, buyers.

Here are some rules to guide you in remembering them:

1. You cannot remember a person's name if you are more interested in what you have to say than what the buyer wants to hear. Be interested in him. Think of him as a personality. If you want to remember his name, you will.
2. Write down the names of your customers and prospective customers – anyone who can help you to get an order. Do it immediately after leaving the shop, office, or factory. Refer to your diary every time you call on that customer, so that you get his name right.
3. Make certain that you know how to spell a name. When you ask a shop assistant for a buyer's name, don't be satisfied with a gabbled answer. Ms McPherson could sound just like Ms Mackeson. Mr Lemm can sound like Mr Lamb. Ask the assistant to spell the name, and then spell it back, to make sure that you have it correctly.

4. Use the buyer's name at least seven times during the sales presentation. Repetition will help to fix it firmly in your memory.

Friendship begins when you remember a person's name.

Tact
No one with prejudices should ever be sent abroad to sell.

These words were used by an export director. She went on to explain that anyone with race or religious prejudices would inevitably reveal them at some time or another, and thus lose orders and, more important, goodwill.

This is true. I have been in many parts of the world and heard of orders lost through the tactlessness of export representatives. The person with strong prejudices usually lacks tact. But tactlessness is not exclusive to this kind of person. Unimaginative people are often tactless, because they do not know they are hurting others. We all make tactless mistakes at some time or another and wish that we had bitten our tongue instead. If we are conscious of this weakness, we can reduce it to the minimum, although we cannot always entirely eradicate it.

To the prejudiced, little advice can be given. They must cope as well as they can with their outlook. To the unimaginative, little help can be given. If a person does not know he is doing wrong, how can he be cured of his faults? But most of us can learn to be more tactful.

Here are a few rules:

> People of all nationalities, colours, and creeds can tell stories against themselves and enjoy them. They do not, however, enjoy the stories of others about their so-called characteristics. Never make sweeping statements like: *I can't stand the French, Australians get me down* or *Americans are a pain in the neck.* You may have disliked an Indian you met, or perhaps a Dutch person has annoyed you, but only a fool would condemn a whole nation because he disapproved of one or two of its people.

Do you want to know whether you are tactless? Ask yourself if you have ever greeted anyone with:

'You're not looking too well!'

If so, you're tactless.

You can change merely by trying not to hurt and upset people. To develop a more friendly personality, be tactful.

Giving Praise

Flattery is no part of a friendly personality. No one wants a friend who always lies – and to flatter is to lie. The fifty-year-old buyer who looks sixty is not taken in if she is told that she looks thirty. She may seem flattered, but she knows it is a lie.

But if she *could* be mistaken for a woman in her early thirties, she cannot be reminded too often. It is the truth and she knows it; her mirror proves it.

People are not charmed when they see through flattery and know it is false.

On the other hand, few people give praise and appreciation where it is due. Husbands find it hard to praise their wives, and wives are tongue-tied at the thought of expressing their apprecia-. tion of their husbands. The managing director won't praise his executive team – the executive team won't praise the office manager – the office manager won't praise the staff. And the staff won't praise anyone. Too many production managers find it easier to criticise a salesperson than praise him, and many a salesperson would rather blow his own trumpet than raise the self-esteem of a customer by praising his display, advertisement, or factory layout.

Why is this? I do not know. Some people will not praise for fear of being thought flatterers. But most are just pig-headed. Praise can make others happy and, if it is withheld, it can turn a warm-hearted person into a sour cynic.

General Smuts said:

> *Praise can bring colour to the drabbest of lives. It can make life worth living, and help a man to succeed.*

It can work wonders for the giver and the recipient. It is as welcome to the successful as the unsuccessful. When a chairman is praised by a newspaper editor for the fine results of his company, he glows with pleasure. I was with one who was singled out for this reason in a leading newspaper. He insisted on ordering champagne all round. Normally, he counts every penny he spends. Would he ever praise another? Never!

I have seen tough newspaper columnists made very happy indeed by praise for their writing – and these are people who like to think of themselves as cynical and hypercritical, never taken in by flattery. But they were delighted by praise they knew to be deserved.

Those who complain bitterly that no one appreciates their efforts are the very people who do not give praise in return.

How often have you heard such remarks as:

'He doesn't appreciate me.'
'They don't know what I do for them.'
'They are never satisfied.'
'You could kill yourself for her before you got a word of praise.'
'He's always grousing – never gives a pat on the back.'

These are typical of people starved of praise. How do you react when someone praises you for work well done? Do you feel annoyed? Do you lose your temper with them? Of course not! You feel all the better for their kind words.

Constant criticism kills ambition, but praise boosts a person's self-esteem, and everyone needs to feel important. Praise everyone who gives you good service. Praise the shop assistant who takes pains to help you. Praise the driver who drives well. Praise the little people. Praise the big people. Praise your customers. Praise your executives. Praise your family . . . But the praise must be merited, and the appreciation honest.

Only the strong person can praise others. The weak person is often niggardly in his praise, because he feels that if he gives it, others will ask favours of him. Praise does not make a person swollenheaded; it helps him to do even better in the future than he has done in the past.

Of all the thousands of people I have met in a long business career, none failed to respond to justifiable praise. Our enemies flatter us, but our friends praise us only when they believe it is honestly deserved. That is why justifiable praise and a friendly personality are linked.

Look and See

How observant are you? Many people look, but see little. The flicker passing across the face when something distasteful is said – the change of expression in a waiter when some buffoon snaps his fingers to attract his attention – the fear in a child's eyes as adults mention gruesome details of an illness – the glint of anger at some tactless remark – the attempt at bonhomie as a disguise for anxiety . . . Only observant people notice these signs and can tread warily, changing the topic of conversation, or giving help where it is needed. It is a standard joke that no husband ever notices his wife's new clothes or hair style. How many family quarrels have been caused by such a failure of observation? Women are usually much more observant than men. Men should strive for more equality of the sexes in this respect.

Before going into a shop, look at the window so that you are familiar with its display. In an office, look for a sign of a hobby or interest: photos, plants, sporting trophies. In a factory, look at the layout *and* the employees. What you observe can help you to get on better terms with the buyer. Notice little things – badges, earrings, nicotine-stained fingers. Notice big things – auto-mation, air conditioning, fork-lift trucks. Observe everything from inter-office telephone systems to the demeanour of a PA when she arrives with a message for her manager.

When you are observant, you can talk in terms of the other person's interests. You can discuss someone's likes and dislikes. You can give praise when it is due. You can avoid making tactless remarks.

Is it hypocritical to develop a friendly personality? Think of it this way: is it hypocritical to be courteous to those who help you? Is it wrong to make people happier by showing appreciation for their actions? Is it wrong to respect all the people who go into the making of a big business?

Your answers to these questions must show you that, far from being hypocritical, it is good to develop a friendly personality.

A SINCERE PERSONALITY

About 350 B.C., Mencius said: *If Heaven wishes that the kingdom should enjoy tranquillity and good order, who is there beside me to bring it about?* And this he set about doing. For more than twenty years, he travelled from court to court in China, lecturing and even ridiculing men in high places. He believed in the principles of benevolence, righteousness, and piety, and the judgment of conscience. He said: *There is no greater delight than to be conscious of sincerity and self-examination.* To search our own souls and find that we have not been motivated by jealousy, envy, and unkindness, that we have acted with sincerity, is indeed a great satisfaction. Sincerity means being genuine, free from prejudice, the same in reality as in appearance.

To look sad on bearing bad news but to be secretly delighted at another's misfortune is the height of insincerity. To both *appear* and *be* concerned is to be sincere. If you are to have a sincere personality, you must pursue an ideal. You must be different from others, who are insincere without knowing it.

Loyalty
The test of loyalty does not come when your affairs are prospering, and when your contribution is being praised. It comes when you are out of favour and your efforts are being frowned upon.

Many salespeople with customers who have complaints blame production managers for what has gone wrong. This is disloyal. Other sales agents speak harshly of their companies, and belittle the efforts of the management. Some criticise their company's product to customers. They would still call themselves loyal.

If a seller cannot be loyal to his firm, he should leave it. If a production manager cannot be loyal to his sales staff, he should be dismissed.

It is not disloyalty to leave a company for better terms and conditions elsewhere. Loyalty does not bind you to one company forever. But so long as you are employed by a company, you must give it your whole loyalty. No one can be sincere and disloyal at the same time.

Be a Good Listener

Most of us talk too much. We think our own conversation so interesting – we know the other person's by heart.

Unfortunately, the other person feels just the same way about us. Doctor Johnson said: *The misfortune of Goldsmith is that he goes on without knowing how to get off.* Does this happen to you? Do you ever go from one subject to another, without knowing when to stop?

Will Rogers said: *A good listener is not only popular everywhere, but after a while he knows something.* When a salesperson listens to a buyer instead of talking all the time, he often learns a great deal.

Are you a pouncer? In other words, do you rarely allow anyone to complete a story? You may be with a friend who is telling you her holiday experiences. She begins, 'I went to the travel agency to book for . . .' Without letting her finish, you interrupt to tell her, 'You should have gone to Boon's – they're the best agents I know. When we went to Italy last year . . .'

Then there's the health pouncer. He says to a friend, 'How are you?' The friend replies, 'Not too well, I'm afraid. I've got . . .' but he is interrupted with, 'Do you know, when I got up this morning, the pain in my back was so bad I just don't know how I carried on . . .'

Sincere people are good listeners. They are sincerely interested in other people.

Wandering Eyes

A rabid talker can be turned into a good listener. If you are in the first category, force yourself to keep silent when someone else is talking. Never interrupt. Never, by gesture or expression, indicate that you are bursting to say your piece. Look as if you are listening. Don't let your eyes wander round the room.

Nothing is more annoying than to know that a listener is only pretending to listen. You may be telling someone in a hotel lounge what is, to you, a most interesting story. Suddenly you realise that she is not listening, but following the movements of everyone passing through the swing doors. She is not even paying you the compliment of pretending to be interested in your story.

Develop the habit of being an intent listener.

Four into One
If you are to have a selling personality, you must combine four personalities. Here they are again:

    a cheerful personality
    a strong personality
    a friendly personality
    a sincere personality.

This chapter has had two aims: the first – to clarify the selling personality, and the second – to convince you that one of a seller's greatest assets is a knowledge of human relations.

2

Conversational Selling

I had not been outstandingly successful and, once more dissatisfied, I heard of a job which seemed worthwhile.

I knew of a Frenchman named Simon who had successfully imported and sold silk materials from Lyons, France. When I heard that he wanted an assistant, I quickly called him and said, 'I should very much like to join you. I have nearly six years of good sales experience, and I am looking for an opportunity of helping to build a big business.'

Mr Simon seemed interested in me, and suggested that, before either of us made a decision, we should spend a day together. I readily agreed.

The following Tuesday morning, I met him at nine, outside John Lewis, the well-known store in Oxford Street, London. Our first call brought a big order, and at other stores Mr Simon was warmly welcomed. He had charm plus a strong personality. All day I listened, and admired.

At five, we had tea and I was anxious to learn whether Mr Simon would engage me. As I had said very little during the day, I wondered how he could judge me. He talked of Paris, the manufacture of silks, of buyers and politics – but not about me. At last I could stand it no longer and I burst out with, 'Mr Simon, I really enjoyed today and know that I can help you. Will you employ me?'

He answered, 'Well, you have found out more about me, but I don't know very much about you. Tell me what you have been doing.'

I told him. I explained how I had started with a tobacco company which *had* to fail, as it was competing with another long-established company. Then I went on to tell him that I had left Company A because they were very old-fashioned and their prices were not competitive; that Company B had not taken my advice to spend more money on advertising and, without advertising, consumer products could not be sold; that Company C had a most difficult sales manager and no one could work with him; that Company D, which sold office machinery, did not have an adequate service staff to back up the sales I had made, and so on. In this way, I catalogued my failures which, up to that moment, I had thought of as my successes. As I finished, Mr Simon said, 'And so, Mr Tack, you have always been right and everyone else wrong.'

At that moment, for the first time in my life, I saw myself as others saw me. The fight left me, and I remember saying, in great humility, 'What, then, is wrong with me, Mr Simon?'

His answer was quite short: 'You are a bad salesman, that's all.'

'But,' I began, 'I have experience, and I have been selling for nearly six years –'

He stopped me. 'Experience does not necessarily teach anyone anything,' he said. 'It can mean a repetition of mistakes. If you had been a good salesman, you would surely have succeeded with one of the companies you have mentioned. Your excuses are used by every salesman who fails. They blame lack of success on some shortcoming of their employers.'

'How then,' I pleaded, 'can I become a first-class salesman?'

'I cannot give you the answer to that,' he replied, 'but most salesmen, both young and old, would improve if they *stopped* selling.'

He was not telling me to get an easier job, but to make a deeper study of the relationship between buyer and seller.

Many salespeople have proudly announced that they have been paid a handsome compliment by a customer. 'Do you know what he said?' one will exclaim. 'He told me I was the best salesperson who had called on him this week!'

In fact, this was an indirect criticism, for the seller must have made it obvious to the customer that he was making an effort to take an order; and this is the worst form of salespersonship.

Selling has been called *the gentle art of giving other people your own way*. That sums it up pretty well.

High-pressure selling is usually fraudulent selling, and an aggressive seller gets nowhere with a professional buyer. Nevertheless, a salesperson must be determined to obtain an order, although the determination mustn't show.

When Mr Simon told me to stop selling, he didn't necessarily mean that I had been too aggressive or too forceful. He meant that I was being too much of a salesperson. I was not being my natural self. My manner and mannerism – my voice and expressions – many of the words I used, were not found in my normal conversation.

What applied to me then applies to many sales agents now. They act like salespeople, they sound like salespeople. They may have the servility of a weak person or the dynamism of a regular quota-buster, but they are frightening the customer. Even top sales agents could improve if they sharpened their selling techniques.

What makes a buyer nervous of a salesperson? When he knows that an attempt is being made to *make* him take a line of action.

But a first-class seller never betrays this determination to the buyer, whether he be managing director, store buyer, production manager, or the owner of a small retail shop. Each buyer likes to feel that she is making her own decision without being swayed by the seller's arguments, but she is swayed, always, by the professional salesperson who sells in a conversational manner.

That is what Mr Simon was trying to tell me.

Market Research

I returned home that evening a very perplexed young man. During the following days, weeks, and months, my brother, who was selling engineering equipment, and I discussed methods of *stopping selling* which would result in more orders.

After a while, we came to this conclusion: whenever we were selling to customers who knew us well and from whom we invariably had orders, we sold to them in a conversational manner, as if they were friends or relatives. There was no need for any personality switch.

From that we concluded that the secret of successful selling was the adoption of a conversational sales presentation. This was the beginning of *conversational selling* – which has since been recognised as the finest form of selling. It is *the gentle art of giving other people your own way* – the most effective way for one person to influence the mind of another.

Having made this important decision, we tried to prove its validity by selling to everyone as if they were friends. We made call after call on difficult customers, but were disappointed that, for all our conversational style, they stayed as difficult as ever. It was quite disheartening, for we had felt so close to a solution to our problems.

We sought again to discover the reason why conversational selling succeeded with buyers who bought from us rather than having to be sold while it failed when the objections came thick and fast. At last we understood that conversational selling relaxed us and this, in turn, relaxed the buyer. We decided that, in spite of our efforts, we did not talk naturally to a prickly customer, because we were too tense and our tension was contagious, so that neither we nor the buyer acted naturally. Our conclusion, which has proved itself correct over many years, was that *a tense buyer never buys*, his tensions being brought about by fear of buying. We knew then that we had to relax in order to sell conversationally and, in so doing, relax the buyer. Many buyers are difficult because they are afraid the seller will dominate them; and tensions are caused by the seller whose forcefulness is *apparent* to the buyer.

A seller of consumer goods employed by the same company for many years might think that he never arouses tensions in his buyers. He is deceiving himself. There are many order-takers in the consumer goods field. They consistently get orders because of the demand for their merchandise, but they would increase sales if they tried to sell when the customer says 'No'.

If the customer doesn't say 'No', no selling is necessary. After taking his usual order, the salesperson might say, 'Mr Jones, you will want to stock up heavily on our new line of detergents. This is a complete breakaway from the usual products and you will benefit in many ways from stocking now, because . . .'

The customer may be stocking all the leading brands and not want any more. For the first time, he will want to see the back of his friend, so he will make excuses such as:

'Leave it for the time being until I've taken stock.'

'I've just had a big delivery of brand XYZ.'

'I have another appointment now, but I'll see you next time.'

If the seller persists, the buyer will tense and may become short-tempered and abrupt, or he may make an excuse and back away.

When a speciality salesperson calls on a prospect for the first time and begins his sales presentation, tension set in immediately. Every good speciality salesperson knows that he must first relax the prospect, right from the opening.

It isn't easy to buy. We are all buyers from time to time. It seems so easy and straightforward to tell a shop assistant that he has nothing to suit us and that we will look elsewhere – but we rarely do it. We make up excuses instead. We pretend that we must match colours, or consult another member of the family, even that we will call back in a short while to make the purchase, when we have no intention of doing so. But when an assistant so obviously attempts to persuade us to buy, we object, and tensions set in.

My brother and I realised that the solution to our problem was first to remove our own tensions. Only then could we sell in a conversational manner, and so relax the buyer.

Learning to Relax

When we decided that the art of selling was to relax the buyer – that conversational selling relaxed the buyer, and that it was only possible to sell conversationally when we relaxed – we studied various methods of relaxation. But the advice given in books and by so-called authorities was contradictory.

One expert said it was essential to relax for at least forty minutes a day. We tried, and gave up. We could not understand our failure then, but now we know that beginners cannot relax for long. Many people stay tense even when asleep, and wake up tired and with a sense of strain. To stay awake, but utterly relaxed, for as long as thirty minutes is impossible for most people.

Another expert recommended a sloping plank for relaxing upon; one must stretch out on it every day, he wrote, with the head lower than the feet. We tried this, but manipulating the plank only brought on tension. Most people become tense if they have to prepare for relaxation.

It seemed to us that the power of the mind, especially the worried mind, was not taken into account. To advise an anxious person that he must make his mind a blank for even ten minutes is to ask the impossible. It is as if a non-swimmer were told that he must plough his way through at least a mile of water in order to swim.

It was this analogy that decided us that, just as a non-swimmer might cover two or three metres before giving up, and then be encouraged to increase the distance gradually, one could learn to relax completely for a few seconds to begin with, and then increase the period.

The more we investigated, the more we found that very few people understood the meaning of relaxation. The physician who advises a patient to relax more is often so tense herself that she takes barbiturates to calm herself at the end of a day. Her advice to the over-tense patient is to find a hobby, go for a holiday, or take up some sport. She forgets that a hobby or sport provides only temporary relief from tensions. I have been addicted to most sports in the past, and now look forward to weekend golf. Golf is great exercise – especially for the middle-aged – but when I look around the club-house at the end of a morning, I cannot say that everyone there is quite relaxed. Many are irritable because of the way they have played.

Learning to relax takes time, but little effort. Many delegates at our courses believed they were completely relaxed, until they were shown that in some circumstances, they could become very tense – for example, when speaking in public. Even though most sales-people attending our courses are highly experienced, they get very nervous and tense if asked to speak in public. The reason for this is that they are inexperienced in speaking from a platform. Should a student be a practised public speaker, he would not mind.

A doctor explains it like this:

> *On being asked to come to the platform to recite, the student's muscles tense. Fear messages rush to the brain and the brain returns these messages to the muscles, which become even more tense. Tense muscles form poisons, which travel through the bloodstream. These cloud the mind, and the thoughts become still more muddled. More messages to the muscles – more tension – more muddle, and so on.*

A seller is usually tense when:

1. He begins his career in selling while selling is unnatural to him. He passes customer after customer before facing one.
2. He calls on a difficult buyer, or much depends on a call.

Many salespeople are unknowingly tense at every call, and these tensions undermine a seller's work in the field.

Enthusiasm and Relaxation

Relaxing does not mean adopting a couldn't-care-less attitude towards the buyer. The relaxed salesperson can be both enthusiastic and inspiring. His mind is clear and so can deal with any objection. Because he feels better, he looks alert and keen. He can also work hard without suffering the stresses and strains of modern business life.

Relaxing Step-by-Step

It takes a long time to learn to relax; there is no short cut. Benefit cannot be derived from relaxation exercises until they have become a habit and this can take from four to six months. Just as we all take up some hobby with tremendous enthusiasm that dies away after a short while, so the seller, when learning to relax, often gives up too quickly.

To learn to sell conversationally, you must follow a few simple exercises day after day, week after week, month after month. That is the way to achieve relaxation. When the time comes and you are in a situation that would normally tense your muscles, you will automatically relax. We found the easy way to relax when we learned that it was impossible to do so for thirty minutes or more at a time. We could relax parts of the body for a minute or so without any trouble. For a minute, the brain can concentrate and the mind will not wander.

HOW TO TRAIN YOURSELF TO RELAX

Relaxing must become a habit. You give so little time to it that it doesn't become a strain or set up negative thoughts. Most people can concentrate for a minute at a time. The first step is to divide the body into seven parts; they are:

> your left arm muscles
> your right arm muscles
> your left leg muscles
> your right leg muscles
> your stomach and chest muscles
> your back muscles
> your face muscles.

Think for a moment of your left arm – that's easy enough, isn't it? Before concentrating your thoughts for one minute on your left arm muscles, you must remember two words. They are not especially original, for they have been used by teachers of relaxation for many years. If you tell yourself to relax, it doesn't have much effect, but if you tell a muscle, or a part of your body, to *let go*, then after a while it does just that – it lets itself go. To anybody who is tense, those with any knowledge of relaxation will say, 'For goodness sake, let yourself go!'

So remember the seven parts of your body, and the two words *let go*.

Now begin the minute technique. Start tonight when you go to bed. Lie flat on your back and for only one minute – it doesn't matter if it is a little less – concentrate all your thoughts on the muscles of your left arm. Tell the muscles to *let go*. Say the word *let* as you breathe in, and *go* as you breathe out. Do that for one minute, and then put relaxation out of your mind.

Next day when you have a little spare time (perhaps after

lunch, or while you are waiting to see someone), concentrate on that left arm again, and once more tell the muscles to *let go*.

Continue for seven days and every night, but not more than three times a day. You will know when the muscles are properly relaxed, because you will get a warm tingling feeling in them.

The Second Week
During the second week, you must concentrate all your thoughts on your right arm – just for one minute, two or three times a day and when you go to bed. Forget all about your left arm. You will find that it will automatically relax itself.

The Third Week
During the third week, carry out the same procedure with your left leg. For this, you must be sitting down, or lying in bed. When sitting, don't cross your legs, but put your feet flat on the ground.

The Fourth Week
For the fourth week, concentrate on your right leg muscles, ignoring your arms and your left leg.

The Fifth Week
The fifth week is given over to your stomach and chest muscles.

The Sixth Week
The sixth week is the turn of your back and shoulder muscles.

The Seventh Week
Your facial muscles take up the seventh week. Your teeth must not be clenched – there must be no wrinkles on your forehead.

Now a warning: don't hurry! Remember, this is a long-term exercise. Spend two weeks on each part of your body if you wish.

Assuming there is good progress, you will relax completely in seven weeks. For the following two or three months, concentrate your thoughts on your entire body, and let all your muscles go – remember, for only a minute at a time. Then you will find, as many others have already, that you will relax automatically. And that was your initial aim.

Only after six months have passed should you try to relax for longer than a minute at a time.

How does this technique differ from others? It makes relaxing an unconscious habit. Make the effort. Don't expect miracles the first week or so. You will not detect much difference for quite a while. Then it happens quickly. Here are the rules again:

1. Remember these seven parts of the body:

    the left arm muscles
    the right arm muscles
    the left leg muscles
    the right leg muscles
    the stomach and chest muscles
    the back muscles
    the face muscles.

2. Remember to lie flat on your back, and the words *let go*.
3. Start with the left arm. Tell the muscles to *let go* and repeat this for one minute. Start tonight when you go to bed. Then repeat it two or three times a day.
4. Concentrate on your left arm alone for the first seven to ten days.
5. After this, concentrate on your right arm and forget your left arm. Carry on for seven to ten days.
6. Concentrate in turn on the remaining five parts of your body, allotting seven to ten days for each part.
7. After two or three months, carry out the same *let go* procedure with your whole body.
8. After six months, practise relaxation regularly, but increase the time to from two to five minutes for each period.
9. You must maintain the short daily relaxing exercises until your muscles respond automatically at the least sign of tension.

The art of good salesmanship is to sell in a *conversational manner*, and when you train yourself to relax, you will begin to sell naturally, and more efficiently.

3

The Value of the Voice

Selling is often made difficult and complicated by the inability of salespeople to communicate effectively. Orders are lost when a buyer:

has difficulty in hearing a seller
misunderstands what a seller has said
loses concentration because of the monotony of a seller's voice.

You must have seen someone being interviewed on television whose immediate good impression was quickly discounted when he started to speak. Many a salesperson, taking great pride in his appearance, his integrity, and his ability to demonstrate, reduces his effectiveness through his inability to communicate and speak with clarity, so that he may be heard and understood.

If you think you may fall into this category, how do you begin to improve your ability to communicate?

You can start by realising that everyone has all the equipment needed to speak well but that very few people learn to use it properly. Making a sound is one of the most natural things we do. Babies make sounds. But shaping sounds into speech is something we all have to learn. So, to begin with, make a sound – any sound. Go on, don't be shy! Did you notice that you breathed out? Now try making a sound as you breathe in. A terrible noise, wasn't it?

Breathing is a vital component of speech. It is the most natural thing we all do, but that doesn't necessarily mean we do it correctly. Most people breathe very shallowly, and quickly run out of breath when speaking for any length of time.

It is just as easy to breathe deeply and, with more breath, you can say, with hardly a pause, quite a long sentence if necessary. Try this: hold your breath as you go on reading. When you can't hold it any longer, let it out, and see what happens. You will notice that it is immediately replaced by quite a deep breath – proving that it is easy, and natural, to breathe deeply. And what is more, it is good for you. With deeper breathing, more oxygen will course around your body and you will feel better and more alert.

Breath is the motive power of sound and is, therefore, vital to speech. As you breathe out, the air leaving the lungs passes up the windpipe and through the larynx to the mouth. In the larynx, sound is born on the quivering *vocal cords*, but, without a column of air coming up the windpipe to carry it onwards, that sound would be still-born. Many people speak very quietly, and this is often because they do not exert enough air pressure to carry the sound. If you are speaking to a group, or in noisy surroundings, you will need to increase the volume of your voice. Don't shout – it's painful and strains the larynx. To increase your volume, increase the air pressure.

A Simple Exercise

Practise varying your volume and controlling the emission of breath with this simple exercise: take a breath and count from one to five, and back to one again, all on one breath. But when you say *one*, let it be only just above a whisper and increase the volume as you go up to *five*. On the reverse journey, you need full power on *five*, then reduce it through *four, three and two*, till *one* is a penetrating whisper which carries right across the room. It isn't as easy as it sounds. Try it. When you can do *one* to *five*, try *one* to *eight, one* to *ten, one* to *twelve* . . . That will be enough to go on with.

Sound, picked up by the breath, is carried into the mouth, where it is amplified and shaped by the use of the tongue, the teeth, the lips, and a mobile lower jaw. Many people are not nearly flexible enough in the mouth. Children twist their mouths alarmingly and pull all sorts of funny faces, until their mothers say, 'You'll get stuck like that one day!' As they get older, they lose the urge to pull faces and their facial masks take on a settled, adult look – to their vocal disadvantage.

When did you last pull a funny face? Try it – it won't hurt! Now try this: open your mouth as wide as you can and say *ah*. Then purse your lips and say *ah*. Try something else. Push your lips flat and spread them to say *ee*. Now purse them again, but this time say *oh*.

Try this several times, running the sounds into each other: *eeyohweeeyohwweeyoh* . . . Can you feel the movement in your face? Can you still feel it once you have stopped?

Practise this exercise to improve your ability to enunciate the vowel sounds correctly. There are around twenty of them in the English language (experts disagree over the precise number) and each has its own mouth position. But most people use only a few mouth positions, and the result is only too audible, in strained, unnatural vowels.

Vowels, of course, are (or should be) pure sounds, but they are interrupted by consonants – p-b-c-t-d and so on – twenty-one of them in the English language.

Most people can enunciate all the consonants quite correctly, although some have difficulty with one or two – *r* is the most common *problem consonant*. If a consonant gives you difficulty, ask your local library for a book containing tongue-twisters, and practise. If that doesn't do the trick, don't be ashamed to put yourself in the hands of a qualified speech therapist. If you can't find one locally, get in touch with your GP, who can recommend one.

No one likes listening to a person who mumbles – and a buyer doesn't *have* to listen, he can easily bring the interview to a close. Mumbling is due either to lack of volume or to sounds not being correctly formed. Consonants are the main offenders. Almost everyone can enunciate consonants correctly, but the sad truth is that many people do not. Taken in isolation, a sound is easy to understand, but when sounds are combined to make words, enunciation errors creep in. I am not suggesting that you develop an ultra-precise *refined* form of speech, but it is fatally easy to go too far in the other direction.

Slurvian
Have you ever heard of *Slurvian*? No, it isn't the language of some

obscure country that you cannot quite locate on the map. *Slurvian* is lazy, ill-formed speech, and everyone can speak it. You can speak *Slurvian* by omitting a consonant. Is it lazy speech or lazy reading to say Febuary instead of Feb*r*uary? It is certainly lazy speech to say *twenny*, instead of *twenty*, and it is very easily done. Prove it for yourself. Say *Twen*. Now stop and think where your tongue is. It's bunched up, isn't it, with the tip touching your upper teeth.

Try it again – *Twen* – and then finish the word *twen-ty*.

Now try it again – *Twen*, omitting the second *t* – *twen-y*. It is easier to say *Twenny*, isn't it? It is also *Slurvian*, because it is lazy speech.

It is *Slurvian* to omit any consonant which ought to be sounded, like the final *g* in huntin', shootin', and fishin'. But there are so many other ways in which it can be spoken.

Changing a consonant is a common fault – *t* altered to *ch*, for example, as in *amacher* and *attichude*. Thirty can easily become thir*d*y, as in the twen*ty*–twenny example, and, again, the addition of an unnecessary, intrusive, linking consonant is wrong. An extra *r* is the most common: I saw-*r*-another old friend yesterday . . . or, law-*r*-and order.

Linking words together may frequently be correct in French and German, but rarely in English. Even worse is the telescoping of words: *lazngenlmn, azamarrafac, festoval* and *awnjoos* are all pure *Slurvian* for *ladies and gentlemen, as a matter of fact, first of all* and *orange juice*.

Vowels, too, can be spoken with a *Slurvian* accent. Golden can be corrupted to gow*l*den, south to *sarth*, or even sar*ff*. Whole syllables omitted give *Slurvian* overtones to many words: vacuum becomes *vacume*, library – *libry*, jewel – *jool*, police – *pleece*, liable – *libel* (which could produce interesting complications of a legal nature, if not sorted out!).

Of course, many words have local variations both of pro-nunciation and of meaning, and national or regional accents can bring an added beauty to the spoken word. So long as lazy enunciation doesn't creep in, they would escape being labelled as *Slurvian*. Henry van Dyck put it this way:

A local accent is like a landed inheritance: it marks a man's place in the world. Of course, you can have too much of it – a man does not need to carry the soil of his whole farm round on his boots.

which sums it up very well. In other words, cherish your accent if you have one, but make sure that other people can understand you.

So, breathing deeply, and avoiding *Slurvian*, speaking sufficiently loudly and clearly, what else is there to say about the use of your voice?

Only that it could be uninteresting – monotonous, even. Obviously, unless your buyer can hear and understand you, there will be little chance of convincing him of the wisdom of buying from you. Unless he is interested, he isn't likely to give you his full attention. He can, of course, lose interest in what you have to say but he can also be put off by a dull, uninteresting voice.

Sound Interesting

What makes a voice interesting? There are several factors, but the most important are its musical qualities and its variety. The musical sound which the voice makes can be divided into pitch and inflection. The pitch of your voice is largely dependent on the length of your vocal cords. Your singing voice (whether you sing or not) will be bass, baritone, tenor, contralto, soprano or alto. Mostly you may use your natural pitch, but occasionally you will want to change pitch, and you can do this naturally (and correctly) or unnaturally (and harmfully). You will remember the advice not to shout when you want to increase volume. Do you remember why? Yes, that's right: because it will strain the larynx. Changing pitch unnaturally does the same thing. You can change the pitch of your voice by tightening up the throat muscles; but don't do so, because it hurts.

To change pitch naturally, you should consider inflection. Inflection is the musical rise and fall of the voice, the range of notes you use. When speaking, very few people use much of a note range – perhaps you know someone who does, and it is captivating to listen to that voice, isn't it? Captivating! Wouldn't

you like your buyers to be captivated by the sound of your voice?
Improve your inflection, and you will be well on the way.

Improving and extending the range of notes you use for speaking is not all that difficult. There are times when even the least
musical of us sings – in the bath, perhaps, or when driving along
early on a bright, sunny morning. In singing, we use many more
notes than when speaking. The secret is to capture a few, and,
with practice, to make your speaking voice more musical.

Start by identifying the approximate centre of your speaking
range. You don't have to be too precise – you will soon know if
you have identified it accurately. If you have a piano, that will be
helpful, but it is not vital. When you have found the centre, count
up the scale, singing one note at a time: one, two, three, and so
on. How high could you go? Now do the same thing down the
scale.

No doubt with practice you could increase the number of notes
used for singing, but let us concentrate on spoken notes. Now you
know how many notes are available to you, try extending a little
way in each direction.

It has been said that the average English person uses only five
notes for most spoken sound, and that if he could only add one at
each end, that would be an increase of 40 per cent – 40 per cent
more musical – 40 per cent more interesting. Surely that makes
the effort worthwhile.

Let us again consider natural changes of pitch. Think back for
a moment to when you were singing those scales. Try them
again, if you wish.

Did you notice that you moved right out of the natural pitch of
your voice? Suppose you are a baritone, you almost certainly
moved right up into the tenor range – right down into the bass.
And you did it naturally.

Practise regularly and you will be able to pitch your voice
exactly where you wish, effortlessly, at will. Perhaps you are
wondering why you should want to be able to change pitch. You
already do so – but probably not often enough, nor intentionally.
But your voice will certainly become relatively high pitched with
fear – or low pitched in sadness. A high-pitched voice often indi-

cates excitement, and when something of great weight and importance is being said, a deep voice sounds appropriate. That is why you need to practise a natural pitch change: so that the pitch is in keeping with the words; so that your voice *sounds right* for the occasion.

Changing the pitch of your voice whenever appropriate helps to add that other important element of a good voice – variety. Volume changes add variety, as does a change of pace. Again, this is only natural, but the change must be *right*.

In conversation, of course, we should change pace in accordance with what we are saying. Perhaps the point you are making is complicated, so slow down; perhaps what you are saying is exciting, and then speed is appropriate.

Emphasis

Have you ever read a passage in a book, then re-read it, changing the emphasis to make the meaning clearer?

In the written word, the author generally leaves the reader to place the stress where he thinks fit. When speaking, however, this is the duty of the speaker.

Do you use emphasis when you are speaking?

Stressing a word achieves two ends. First, it identifies the important word in a sentence – the word which the listener will remember because the speaker has made him register it more strongly: 'I would recommend the *green* one.'

Second, emphasis changes meaning. Read this sentence, and stress each word in turn. See how the meaning is altered:

> *I* have booked your plane home = *I* did it, no one else.
>
> I *have* booked your plane home = affirmation – Oh yes, I *have* . . .
>
> I have *booked* your plane home = definition – not provisionally, but *firmly* booked.
>
> I have booked plane *your* home = whose? *Yours* but not your colleague's.
>
> I have booked your *plane* home = how? You are not travelling by train.

I have booked your plane *home* = I haven't handled the outward trip.

Closely allied to emphasis and often used with it is the pause. A brief pause before or after the emphasised word will give it additional weight: 'I would recommend the (pause) green (pause) one.'

Of course, you will need to pause for other reasons. Think how a comedian pauses before delivering his punch-line. Why? To make sure that his audience is ready for the laugh, and to add a little drama. There are two points here: always make sure that your buyer can keep up with you, by talking at a restrained pace; but even then it helps to pause occasionally, because the listener can easily get left behind. Pause also for dramatic purposes – to add extra value to your words.

You Can Improve your Voice

If you want to improve the use of your voice, you can certainly do so. Use variations of pitch and pace; introduce inflection, emphasis, and the pause; but, perhaps above all, make sure that you speak with emotion.

You must have watched the classic scene where a producer, rehearsing actors for a play, says wearily, 'Once more – with feeling!' Too often, the feeling is lacking. How often has someone said to you, 'Good morning, may I help you?' with so little emotion that you feel the last thing they want to do is bother with you?

Lack of emotion is fatal to a seller. How can a buyer be impressed by the person who says, 'This is a wonderful machine,' in a dull, lacklustre voice?

Every salesperson knows she must believe in what she is selling, but her belief must be transmitted to the buyer through the feeling in her voice. Sincerity and enthusiasm – those prime qualities of a seller – must be *heard* by the buyer. The right words are not enough – they must be said in an infectious way, sincerely and enthusiastically. Everyone has the ability to do this. It is a sad fact that many people fail to recognise how much effect – for good or ill – their voices can have on their listeners.

You do not need to cultivate the beautiful, resonant tones of the classical actor, but as a seller you certainly do need to recognise how vital a part your voice plays and strive to make it a truly effective tool of your selling.

4

Selling by Objectives

One of the most dynamic influences in commercial and industrial growth occurred with the introduction of Management by Objectives. MBO, as it became known, emphasises the need for each person within a working group to be given his own objective which, added to those of his colleagues, leads to the achievement of the group objective.

The MBO concept is based on the fact that people work more effectively when they know precisely what they are trying to achieve. We have always known, at TACK, that this applies particularly to salespeople. For years, every salesperson in TACK was given set targets – call target, sales targets, targets for the number of appointments made by telephone, number of orders per quotation ... Those attending our courses were given targets according to the specific requirements of their work.

When MBO emerged as a major management technique, I realised that target setting was not enough. Targets, or objectives, should not relate to the direct sales effort alone. They should be segmented. Each day, a seller should have a number of clearly defined objectives, ranging from knowing the best possible selling or demonstration kit to the closing of an order.

With the advent of MBO, we changed the title of Target Selling to Selling by Objectives.

Salespeople went from strength to strength as they appreciated the part each minor objective played in the reaching of the final objective – the order. Although the list of selling objectives is long (pre-planning itself is an objective), salespeople are primarily concerned with call objectives.

Before every call, a seller must always have in his mind a clear objective. Otherwise, he will lack purpose, arouse no interest, and influence no one.

Here are examples of call objectives other than the closing of orders:

Visiting a Production Plant
Joan Wilson, a salesperson for Lancing Ltd, decided that she would achieve a major step towards finalising an order if she could persuade Mr Brown, a production manager and a potential buyer, to visit the Lancing production plant.

What, then, is the objective?

On the face of it, it is simply *to arrange a visit by Mr Brown to the plant.*

But is that the true objective? Joan Wilson is not offering Mr Brown a conducted tour of the plant, but Joan could place the emphasis on the *visit* rather than on the *reason for the visit* when seeing Mr Brown, and that could lose her the order.

At the interview, Joan might say something like this:

> 'You could see the Acme for yourself if you visited our factory, Mr Brown. Of course, I would pick you up in the car, take you to the airport and accompany you to Manchester. One of our executives would meet the plane, you could have lunch with our directors, and this would give you the opportunity to . . .'

Would that travelogue necessarily persuade Mr Brown to visit the factory? Maybe. But possibly he might be concerned about the hospitality and feel that if he made the journey, he might be committing himself to buy.

The emphasis, then, should not be on the *visit*, but the *benefits* Mr Brown will derive from making that visit.

What, then, is Joan's objective? First she must ask herself these questions:

Q. What is the reason for inviting Mr Brown to the plant?
A. Not to see the Acme in operation, but to see for himself the special features of the Acme – features which will be of direct interest and benefit to Mr Brown.
Q. Why should Mr Brown give up his time to make the long journey to Manchester?

A. Because at Brown's production plant they have a problem, and the Acme can be operated by one person only. Also, Acme operators can be taught in three hours how to use the equipment to the best advantage. Mr Brown would be able to satisfy himself on this point because training schools are in progress all the time.

Joan Wilson now has a clear idea of her objective:

> *That Mr Brown should prove for himself the benefits offered by Acme units.*

You will see how the emphasis has changed. No longer is Joan deeply concerned about travel arrangements or the hospitality at the factory. Her objective is to persuade Mr Brown that it is worthwhile putting himself out to see the Acme. *It is incidental that the Acme is at the Lancing plant; it could be anywhere.*

Joan Wilson, knowing her true call objective, will be much more convincing in her arguments, and Mr Brown will be motivated to travel for the *right* reasons.

Dealing with a Complaint

One of your customers may be upset because he feels he has been let down (late delivery, wrong demand for settlement of an account, bad service). You have to call on him to straighten things out.

At first you might consider that the objective is to *deal with an objection*, but on reflection you may decide that a more correct objective would be to *restore confidence and to make sure of continuity of business.*

Your next task would be to set down minor objectives, which could be:

1. To discover the true reason for the complaint and whether or not it is justified. (Many complaints are wrapped up in side issues, generalisations, and reminders by buyers of what happened some years ago – all of which confuse the issue. On the company side, staff often try to justify their own mistakes.)

2. To find out how you can put matters right. (Is a company policy involved? Can extra credit be given? Can free service be given?)
3. To consider ways of ensuring that a similar complaint does not arise again.
4. To rebuild the buyer's confidence in the company.

The final proof that all minor objectives and the call objective are achieved will be evinced when the buyer places further orders with you.

Remember that there are two core types of objectives: 1) decision-based objectives (i.e., to obtain a decision to go forward), and 2) information-seeking objectives (i.e., to obtain information necessary to progress the sale professionally).

Here are some typical specific call objectives:

- to obtain the payment of an overdue account, and retain the goodwill of the customer
- when taking a quotation to a buyer, to pinpoint special features which cannot be offered by competitors
- to obtain information before seeking an interview with the buyer to discover the true reason why an order is being held up
- to survey premises prior to quoting
- to obtain co-operation for new merchandising schemes, sales promotions, local advertising, etc.

Selling by objectives enables a seller to focus her mind on the real purpose of a call. Once that has been determined, the interview with the buyer is not clouded by side issues, making it easier for her to obtain a favourable decision.

5

Buyer Analysis

The potter moulds clay and the sculptor fashions marble, but the seller changes people – calming the irascible, getting the attention of the inattentive, and turning buyers' 'No's' into 'Yes's'. Each day, salespeople motivate people, and the importance of a salesperson preparing for every human contingency cannot be over-emphasised. Salespeople do not have to be psychologists to appreciate that Carl Jung's theory applies especially to buyers.

Jung divides people into three psychological categories:

> *thinking*
> *feeling*
> *intuitive*.

Let us forget people generally, and consider the application of Jung's theory to buyers.

The first type of buyer is logical in his thinking. He will immediately condemn a seller who exaggerates, cannot substantiate a claim, or talks on and on without making a definite point.

Here is an example of a *thinking* buyer:

One of our sales staff called on the buyer for one of the largest hotel chains. Her purpose was to explain why prices had to be increased. The buyer said, 'Your competitor called yesterday and quoted the same service figure as previously. In view of salary increases and inflation, I knew that this was not possible unless their service suffered. I don't like paying extra, but I like bad service even less.'

We got the order.

The *feeling* type of buyer, while still requiring facts, will also respond emotionally to a salesperson's appeal. He is not so cold and calculating as the *thinking* buyer.

An example of the *feeling* type of buyer was provided by a delegate at one of our sales training courses. He said, 'I was explaining the benefits and virtues of a chemical for use in his manufacturing process, but making little headway. Then I told him that the chemical neither polluted air nor water. This immediately aroused the buyer's interest. Apparently he is a very keen fisherman and hates to think of the fish being destroyed by polluted water. His whole manner changed from then on.'

The *intuitive* buyer believes that he has an extra sense – some insight which allows him to arrive at correct decisions more often than others not gifted with his type of intuitive mind.

It isn't always easy for a salesperson to recognise which type of buyer he is dealing with on a first call, but, after several calls, he will be able to type the *thinking, feeling*, or *intuitive* buyer, and vary his sales techniques accordingly.

Although the features of a product do not vary, the words used for expressing these features should change, according to the buyer's mentality and the kind of appeal most acceptable to him.

Managing Directors

Having segregated buyers into their categories, next there must be consideration of the idiosyncrasies of managing directors, the reasons for their actions, and the parts they play in the scene of the industrial theatre.

When selling capital goods, managing directors are often directly involved and, in the medium-sized or smaller companies, they are usually closely concerned with every aspect of buying. Some managing directors – especially the entrepreneurial types – when buying in association with others (directors, managers, committees) highlight their own importance in several ways:

1. *The self-effacing.* This type of managing director conveys the impression that she is listening carefully to the views of her colleagues, but in point of fact her mind can well be made up very early in the salesperson's presentation. Her thoughts are: *Let the others talk – I'll come in at the proper time to make the most impact.* The seller should refer to her continually throughout the presentation.

2. *The self-denigrating.* She will often say, 'I delegate, and forget. This isn't really my concern, you know' – when, of course, everyone knows that it is her concern and that she is the decision-maker. The seller takes a risk when he believes this manager and concentrates on the subordinates.

3. *The strong manager.* This type is brusque to the point of rudeness Her sentiments are: *I'll show everyone around here who's boss!* This is usually an act, and need not frighten the salesperson.

4. *The kind and friendly.* This managing director knows his own importance, and can be very friendly. No salesperson should attempt to take advantage of his attitude, and become familiar.

5. *The short and sharp.* He will say, 'Remember, I'm a very busy man – as are my associates – so don't waste our time.' He will listen for hours if the seller has marshalled her facts and presents them correctly, but will cut the salesperson short if the presentation becomes repetitive.

6. *The sharpshooter.* This managing director constantly interrupts the seller when in full flight; she has a very quick mind and is usually ahead of the salesperson in her thinking. When selling to the sharpshooter, the seller should curtail his sales presentation, keep only to facts, and never, never exaggerate.

These people's attitudes should not be misunderstood. They are usually able – sometimes brilliant – and generally very like-able people but they have to emphasise their own importance. This is a fundamental fact of human relations applicable to many people – as much to Prime Ministers as to production supervisors – to sales directors and their sales staff. A managing director may control 20,000 people and a turnover of £500,000,000, but he can still be unsure that everyone realises how important he is. Why else do leaders of this calibre drop names, refer to calls made upon their time by government departments, and yearn for decorations or titles? Others show photographs of their dogs (making sure the country house is well pictured in the background).

Before employees say, 'Typical of top brass!', they should realise that they are not exempt from the need to feel important.

They, too, put over the same act as the rest of us. Although, so far, we are considering selling to managing directors, it is worthwhile emphasising that a prime lesson for all salespeople is that almost everyone likes to build his own importance.

The seller who is genuinely interested in the work of a factory worker, for example, shows his concern for that worker's skills and the importance of the job he is doing, and will make him feel better. And when the buying decision is made, the advice of the factory worker may well be sought. The salesperson who seeks the advice of shop assistants or is building their importance.

While the amateur seller always builds up her own standing in an attempt to outrival the knowledge of a buyer, the *professional salesperson* will always show strength by making it obvious that she realises the importance of the other person's position. She is right, because everyone involved in the buying decision has a vital task to fulfil, and this should be acknowledged by the seller. Many, many orders have been lost through lack of understanding of this simple aspect of human behaviour, which seems to be inherent not only in managing directors, but in all of us – the need to feel important

Finally, remember that the vast majority of managing directors are not ruthless people. They will always try for a better bargain, but if you have offered the best terms, your product is competitive, and you stand firm by your rights, you will win many more times than you lose. Managing directors do respect the ability of others, which means they respect the *professional salesperson.*

The Unmentionable Buyer

Over the years there has been, on occasion, wide press coverage of events leading up to the trial of someone accused of accepting bribes for giving preferential treatment to a supplier, builder, architect, or local government official. There is such publicity because bribery in industry is so rare. There will always be an occasional crooked buyer, as there are crooked doctors, solicitors, police officers, etc. – but there are very, very few tainted people in the professions or under government employ, and the same applies to industry.

The reason why bribery seems to be rampant is because sales staff *and* production managers have to find excuses for failure.

When a salesperson loses an order he feels certain he should have had, he will say, '*Everyone knows* that X (the buyer) is on the make.' The key word is *everyone*. Whenever anyone wants his statement to be accepted as true, he will begin:

> '*Everyone knows* . . .' or
> '*Everyone says* . . .' or
> '*This is on very good authority* . . .'

But these words are only a camouflage for rumour. No one can ever pinpoint the *everyone*.

If you fail to get an order, try to find out the *real* reason – you can be assured, whatever rumours abound, it will be rarely, if ever, bribery.

Entertaining

Another subject which must be included in buyer analysis is entertaining. We hear stories of buyers having wild nights with call girls, fêted on yachts, or holidaying in Mediterranean châteaux owned by company managing directors. Again, these facts are rarely substantiated. For the majority of salespeople, entertaining *can* cement a friendship, and does allow a buyer to talk over his problems and conduct negotiations away from a busy factory or office, where there may be constant interruptions. Entertaining at this level is not unethical. No buyer is going to place an order just because a seller has bought him dinner. Only if the quality of a product is right, competitive on price, service, etc., and is what the buyer needs, does friendship play a part in selling. When it doesn't matter to the buyer whether he places an order with company A, B, or C, it is the salesperson with the closest relationship with the buyer who will nearly always get the order. Entertaining can help cement that relationship.

But entertaining must be kept in perspective. It might be right for a managing director to take another managing director or chief executive to Claridge's or the Dorchester. It is rarely necessary for a seller to entertain at this level.

I should now like to destroy the myth that all chief executives eat like gourmets and drink only the finest wines. I suppose I have been dined out by, or have dined, as many chairmen and managing directors of companies as anyone. I can count on the fingers of one hand the number who ate anything but sparsely, and the majority drank very little, if any, alcohol.

The buyer knows that the meal is on the company expense account, so it is of little use to act the part of a millionaire to try to impress him. Many, many buyers and those who can influence orders prefer lunch at the local pub to a dinner at an expensive restaurant. Buyers do like a seller who acts naturally, and they do not like to see money thrown away.

There are, of course, the exceptions, but these exceptions who want lavish treatment are rarely influenced by a salesperson, who is generally no closer to the order at the end of the meal than at the beginning. Never believe the promises of this type of buyer. He forms no real friendships, in spite of heavy entertaining – he has been taken out so often and cannot buy from everyone. You lose nothing with this person by not taking him out at all.

To sum up the position: except for the tiny minority who look forward to being fêted, the majority of buyers, ranging from young, highly skilled university-trained technicians to middle-aged production chiefs, from development engineers to project engineers, while enjoying being entertained, do not look for lavishness. These conclusions were substantiated by a TACK survey. *Entertain sensibly – it can cement a friendship.*

DIFFICULT BUYERS

Most buyers are reasonable people who can be influenced by a good sales presentation and by human relations. Some will order; others will have different reasons for refusing to buy. Few salespeople take large orders from everyone they call upon. But the main difference between the good and the average seller is that the first-class seller gets extra orders from customers with whom the average salesperson can make little headway.

With these difficult prospects and customers, the average seller will fail more frequently than he will succeed, because he won't know how to win them over to his side. Even the very experienced representative must work much harder for his orders when a buyer does all he can to put him off.

Why are some buyers so difficult?

The main reason is fear of salespeople, allied to fear of making a mistake. To frustrate a seller, a buyer develops an act.

When you meet difficult buyers, you must be prepared to handle them correctly.

The Talkative Buyer

This buyer's defence mechanism is his ability to out-talk the most verbose salesperson. The sales offer quickly gets bogged down, and if the buyer has her way, never emerges. Not only does she continually elaborate on a train of thought, but interrupts a seller to tell a long and involved story with only a slight bearing on the salesperson's argument. The talkative buyer will sidetrack the salesperson in many ways. She will speak about left-wing or right-wing politicians, problems with the Euro, the difficulties of management, sport, her staff, or her hobbies. She will also like to reminisce – 'I remember once, when I was offered . . .' or, 'Of course, you know Brown & Co. Well, I remember when they first made . . .'

After some ten minutes of chat, this buyer will often say, 'Well, thanks for calling. I'm afraid I'm rather busy this morning. Can you leave that brochure (sample, brochure, photograph, etc.) and I'll be in touch.'

The interruption technique is the best way of selling to the talkative buyer. The seller should interrupt when she can do so without being discourteous. For example:

> 'That is a most interesting point you've made, Mrs Smith. There's too much form-filling in business today. That is why . . .'

or

> 'Mrs Smith, forgive me for interrupting you, but what you
> have just said is vital to retailing, because . . .'

This technique is usually acceptable, but it can falter if the
seller is half-hearted in her interruption. She must speak strongly,
and then immediately revert to her sales offer.

Once the talkative buyer listens to a seller without constant
interruptions, she can be involved in the real purpose of the call.

The Too-friendly Buyer

A buyer may be abrupt, curt, almost rude, but he may also listen
carefully to a salesperson's proposition. The brusque buyer is not
too difficult a person to overcome, but the too-friendly buyer can
make life very hard for the seller.

He seems to agree with everything, but still doesn't buy. This
buyer greets a sales agent pleasantly, but this is a disguise. He
knows it is hard for sales staff to *sell* when he is being so friendly.
The timid seller is always impressed with friendliness, and will
write on his report to head office:

> 'Mr Brown greeted me in a most friendly way. He listened
> to everything I had to say and agreed with our proposition.
> He would not come to an immediate decision but he is,
> undoubtedly, a very good prospect. I feel sure that next time
> I call I shall get an order.'

But he won't get an order. The buyer will be just as friendly on
the next occasion, saying, 'I told you last time that I like your
product, but I'm not quite ready for it.'

To tackle a friendly buyer needs strong will power. If the buyer
agrees, the strong salesperson will immediately ask for the order.
The friendlier the buyer becomes, the stronger, in the gentlest
but firmest way, the seller sells. He knows the buyer for what he
is worth, and will not be shown to the door with the buyer's arm
around his shoulders and a 'thank you for calling'. The only
thanks he wants for calling is the signed order.

A buyer's friendship is proved when he gives you orders.

The Buyer Who Is Scared of Buying

With a scared or timid buyer, confidence-building must have a high priority in the sales offer. This buyer won't buy unless he has complete confidence in a supplying company. For this reason, it is wrong to ask the timid buyer for his advice – something that most buyers appreciate. He will consider it a sign of weakness and will conclude that the sales agent is not competent.

With this buyer there must be no equivocation; no alternative should be offered. The sales agent should determine exactly what he wants the buyer to buy, and then keep to that decision.

This buyer, is so afraid of making a mistake, but probably the real mistake was in placing him in the position of having to make buying decisions. There are many first-class project engineers, production managers, office managers, quite capable of running their sections efficiently, but still afraid of making buying mistakes.

A scared buyer often works for a tough boss, which could be one of the reasons why he is afraid of making a decision. The salesperson selling to this buyer must remember that *there is nothing so contagious as enthusiasm* except the lack of it

Once confidence has been established, the enthusiasm of a seller can inspire the scared buyer to overcome his fears and become equally enthusiastic about a product or service.

But a word of warning. This buyer is difficult to recognise at a first call; he may even look tough and determined, but it is a rough exterior hiding a quaking stomach. His standard ploy to get rid of a sales agent is, 'I'll have to put this before . . .'

Of course he could make the decision himself, but he can't rid himself of his fear of his chief. Once the salesperson has built up trust in himself and his company, he will find that the scared buyer can be very loyal to him.

The Taciturn Buyer

This buyer is the opposite of the compulsive talker. She says little, often signalling acquiescence by a grunt rather than a 'Yes', which she feels doesn't commit her so much. This taciturn person is usually introspective and almost the perfect listener – except

that her listening doesn't seem to bring her any nearer to arriving at a decision, and she doesn't help the seller by talking much herself.

There is a similarity between her and the compulsive talker, because the technique for selling to her is similar. To involve the non-talker in the sale, a salesperson must ask a series of questions. Adroit questioning will force the silent buyer to become involved in the sale, if the questions are directly pertinent to the buyer's business. The seller will find that the silent buyer will answer them, possibly at length, and the seller knows that he will be able to complete his sales offer with the buyer involved.

The Bluffer

These memos to a sales manager at head office are the results of a sales agent calling on the *Bluffer*:

Memo 1.

I was with Mr Evans today. He wants us to quote for 160 Sponlites Mark II. He didn't seem at all worried about the cost – he knows the total order with spares will be in excess of £30,000.

Memo 2.

Mr Evans is very interested in the quotation – thank you for getting it through so quickly. He now wants an amended quote for 110 Sponlites Mark II, and 80 Sponlites Mark III. Naturally, I am delighted as this will substantially increase the order. It will be the largest I have ever taken, and I know that he is not even going to Hardwicks for a quote.

Memo 3.

I took the revised quote to Mr Evans but he was too busy to see me. However, he left a message to say he would telephone.

Memo 4.

I saw Mr Evans today. He is very impressed with the quote, the layout and the drawings, which he thought excellent. I have to call next week.

Memo 5.

Mr Evans told me that, as the order is in excess of £40,000,

it has to be finally sanctioned by the Board, but he says that
will cause no problem.

Memo 6.

Mr Evans away on holiday.

Memo 7.

Bad news, I'm afraid. The Board have refused to sanction
the order because of the credit squeeze, but Mr Evans
assures me that I have nothing to worry about. The order
will be ours as soon as the squeeze is lifted.

Memo 8.

I am sorry to have to tell you that Mr Evans has installed six
Donolites (Hardwicks' product). This really shook me until
he said that I was not to worry – the big order will be ours
when . . .

The never-ending saga of the salesperson who believed the
Bluffer – the buyer who thinks big but buys small.

The Bluffer misleads a seller in another way when he says, 'I
never play about. It's either the lot or nothing for me! We'll
replace all the telephones or none at all – and I want to do the
whole job.'

The seller feels that he is winning, and the buyer continues:
'But this all ties up with other top management plans, so come
back and see me in about six months' time and then I'll be ready
to talk business.'

The seller goes away starry-eyed, convinced that he will get a
big order in six months' time.

The way to tackle this buyer is to try to give him what he really
wants, without cutting him down to size. The sales agent might
say to the buyer interested in telephones, 'Mr Brown, I
appreciate that you will want to install about two hundred
telephones to cover the whole building, but I would like to
suggest that you do the corner block first. Some of our biggest
accounts started with us by testing our claims for themselves and
subsequently they all switched over completely. Now that will
only mean an initial outlay of . . .'

The seller has called the Bluffer's bluff without the Bluffer
being aware of what has happened. Telling him that some of the

largest organisations (he might even mention one or two of them) have started purchasing your telephones for one section of their premises coincides exactly with what the Bluffer had been thinking. There is always the strong possibility with the Bluffer that by suggesting a small order to begin with, the sale will be made.

This seems to go against all selling principles. Many salespeople will hold up their hands in horror at the thought of taking a small order instead of a large one. This is the snag. How do you recognise the Bluffer? First, if he has played the game with you before; secondly, he sometimes gives himself away by his apparent eagerness to buy big. While the person who buys big goes very closely into every aspect of a proposition, the Bluffer doesn't question, and question again, the seller's claims.

BUT

if there is the slightest doubt in your mind – if you are not at least 90 per cent sure you are being bluffed, then you must go out for the big order.

If you have been bluffed once, you will know better next time.

The Stubborn Buyer

When the stubborn buyer has made up his mind, nothing seems to budge him. Any hint of criticism will lose the order. He would rather make a wrong decision than change his mind. His problem is psychological – he is afraid of appearing weak. He is the kind of person who will tell you that he always believes in admitting when he is in the wrong; unfortunately, he always believes he is right. The strength of your sales presentation enables you to sell to him. If he has raised an objection, he doesn't like to be proved wrong.

A presentation that forestalls objections lets him feel he is making all the decisions all the time.

The Busy Buyer

You know how it is in offices when the boss walks in – all the staff, even those who have nothing to do, act as if the work is really piling up for them. Do they mislead their boss? Not at all! But both sides enjoy the act.

It's no different with the busy buyer. He is not overworked, either, but when a sales agent calls, he is confronted with a scene of such activity that he believes it hardly worthwhile mentioning the reason for his call.

Remembering the axiom *never attempt to sell under adverse conditions*, the seller excuses himself for interrupting the buyer while he is so busy and leaves, with the buyer assuring him that he will see him some time later. But the seller may have overlooked the corollary to the axiom: *but be sure that the conditions are adverse – don't jump to conclusions.*

It is so easy to believe that you are being confronted with an adverse selling situation when, in reality, the buyer is always on the go and, therefore, whenever you call, the situation will be no different, or will go into his busy buying act especially for your benefit.

Generally, the busy buyer doesn't use his act as a defence against sales agents. He just likes to give everyone the impression that he works twenty-four hours a day at top speed, all the time. And if this enables him to get rid of unwelcome visitors, so much the better.

Look for these signs when meeting the busy buyer for the first time:

1. A constantly ringing telephone.
2. He tells you he must make a telephone call before the interview begins.
3. Interruptions from his staff.
4. He examines papers while you are talking, mumbling something about always having to do two things at a time.
5. He leaves the office or shop, saying, 'Excuse me, I've just got to see about a delivery – be back in five minutes.'

There are two ways of tackling the busy buyer. He must be interested quickly in the seller's proposition, and that interest must be maintained. Also, the salesperson must let the buyer know that he is impressed by the scene of activity.

The seller might say, 'Mr White, how do you keep up this pace?'

This will enable the buyer to say what his reasons are for being so busy: lack of staff – tremendous pressure of work – 'it's the way I'm built'. But while he is talking, the salesperson will notice that he is beginning to slow down, because he is talking about one of his favourite subjects – himself. This will relax the busy buyer, who will enjoy impressing the salesperson with his ability to do the work of three men. Once having established this point, the busy buyer is often prepared to sit back and listen to the salesperson.

Mr/Ms Pompous

There are pompous people everywhere, but some buyers are so self-important that they are more pompous than most. They are conscious of their authority, and their hold over a seller; they have him at their mercy. They are often fawned upon by weak salespeople. They are tin gods of their little empires. They enjoy showing off to the staff at the expense of the sales agent.

If Mr Pompous should be a factory manager, he struts among the machinery in his workshops, his every step indicating his sense of his own importance.

You cannot win over this prospect by deflating him, by making him appear unimportant. A seller cannot diminish him by building himself up, by pointing out that other firms place large orders for his goods. This makes the prospect feel less important, and antagonises him because he cannot equal those big orders. And if you deflate him you are finished. You must build him up. Congratulate him on the way his department or shop is run, if it is well administered. If he is known as a keen buyer, tell him that everyone knows he is a keen buyer. If he will often make a quick decision, tell him that he has the reputation of a man who, once he has made up his mind, will take action and buy. If you can give him *honest* praise and appreciation, to convince him that you share his belief in himself, you should do so.

Mr/Ms Shy

Someone who buys regularly might be expected to lose all sense of shyness, but many buyers are shy.

The shy buyer will seldom look you in the face, and his eyes will wander disconcertingly around the room. He must be closely involved in the sale and this can be done by asking questions, or by using pencil and notepad. As you develop your sales presentation, write down some of the features, and show them to the buyer for his agreement. If calculations are required, make them with the shy buyer – such co-operation will help to overcome his shyness.

The Sarcastic Buyer

The sarcastic buyer may have a warped sense of humour, or a difficult home life. If so, she may boost her authority by sarcasm towards sales agents and colleagues. She delights in making the seller feel small. She comments caustically upon your sales kit, your company – salespeople in general. She interrupts your sales presentation with some foolish remark that may raise a laugh from one of her assistants.

She is at the top of her form with an audience: an assistant buyer, shop assistant, her colleagues; she loves playing to the gallery. If you quarrel with her, you will lose the account for good. You will be sorely tempted to do so, but a seller should subdue such reactions against a prospective buyer. At all costs, keep your temper. Try to smile at her sarcasm; explain that you know how she feels about the company, but she is not quite correct because . . . She is showing off, and probably using sarcasm in self-defence.

Ms Sarcastic may not be a bad person underneath, and, if you persist without losing your temper, you will eventually get an order. She won't stop being sarcastic, but her remarks will lose their sting when you get to know her better.

The Old and Experienced Buyer

He will probably have been in business for many years, either on his own account or for others. He may not take kindly to new ideas, and he doesn't think highly of modern salesmanship. He lives in the past – when he could, with more leisure, select the goods he required. He is often a kind person and, while he may seem irritable occasionally, put it down to his having heard everything before, or to his health being less good than it once was. He always believes that the seller is trying to put something over on him; talking down to him will lose any chance of an order.

Do not be clever with this buyer. Never produce the quick answer. You must respect him for what he is, and for what he has done. You may not see eye-to-eye with him, but he has vast experience in his line of business. Learn from that experience.

Ask his advice. Show him that you are ready to learn from him much more than he can learn from you. Impress him with your integrity and honesty. Never try to rush him, or force an issue. Prove each point, step by step. Do not judge him by appearances – he is not like the sarcastic buyer. He may look gruff and frightening, but he could develop into a great friend.

The Young Buyer

This is a most difficult buyer – the youngster who has risen too quickly. She hates you to think her young and inexperienced; she is scared of making a mistake that would prompt a relative or superior to wonder if it was right to give such a young person an important position.

One day she will learn her business and carry out her job efficiently. Now it is your duty to help her, by giving her a complete sales presentation and so teach her about your products; she then learns more about the goods she is buying.

If you are older, take care to show her the greatest courtesy and do not imply that your experience is superior to hers. At the same time, let her teach you something so that you can thank her for her help. You must make her feel less young and inexperienced. This way you will sell to her, and make a good friend of her.

KNOW YOUR BUYERS

To understand the buyer is to understand yourself. Most of us, at some time or another, have acted a part when buying.

Ask yourself these questions:

When in a shop, have I ever said, 'I have an appointment, so I shall have to call back and try it on later?'

Or you may be looking at a piece of furniture in a shop costing perhaps £1,000, but you only want to spend £500. On such an occasion, have you ever said to your partner, 'Well, it would go very well in our dining room', when you haven't the slightest intention of paying £1,000 for that piece of furniture?

Or when your partner insists that you visit a showroom to look at a new refrigerator which you don't want to buy, have you acted the part of the taciturn buyer, just answering in monosyllables?

And, when buying a car, have you shown off to the assistant by rattling off all you know about fuel injection or computerised engine-management systems?

You may not be able to identify with these scenarios, but if you think hard enough, you will remember the occasions when you have been the too-busy buyer, the silent buyer, the stubborn, or the talkative buyer . . .

When we understand the parts we play when considering a purchase, we shall more readily understand that professional buyers are no different from us. Some days they feel well and on other occasions they are below par.

Some days their responsibilities lie very heavily upon them, and this shows, while on other occasions, when everything is running smoothly, they will act differently towards you.

A professional seller soon recognises all the signs, and acts accordingly.

When you recognise the parts the buyers play, you will have made your first step towards motivating them to listen AND be interested in YOU.

6

Buyer Motivation

To be certain that his offer has the right appeal, a seller must understand the reasons behind a buying decision – what motivates a buyer. Is it price – quality – confidence in a supplier? It could be any or all of these reasons, and selling would be easier if buying motives could be isolated as simply.

To understand motives, it is easier to begin with fundamentals. Here are reasons, taken from biographies and autobiographies, which have motivated people to explore:

Explorer A: 1. *Main Motive:* To discover rare plant specimens
     2. To discover physiological and psychological limits
     3. To test endurance

Explorer B: 1. *Main Motive:* To win applause by conquering the unconquerable
     2. To discover oneself

Explorer C: 1. *Main Motive:* To contest previous theories about the origin of a tribe of people
     2. To write a book

Explorer D: 1. *Main Motive:* For fun
     2. To make a film for television so that others might share your enjoyment of something

Explorer E: 1. *Main Motive:* To get away from a humdrum existence
     2. To prove to family and friends that one is different from others
     3. To seek a quiet existence
     4. Revulsion against overcrowded modern cities
     5. To find out whether Robinson Crusoe could exist under modern conditions on an uninhabited island

On the face of it, the main objective of Explorer A was to seek rare plant specimens, but perhaps what finally convinced him that he should take risks financially and physically was the need to test himself – to discover his physiological and psychological limits.

Explorer E yearned to get away from a humdrum existence, but she was also motivated by a need to achieve some inner peace in the security of life on an island, and to be unique.

The lessons to be learned from these examples of motivation are these:

1. There is usually a main motive and subsidiary motives behind every human action.
2. A motive which influences one person may not apply to another, although both may have dual objectives.

These facets of human behaviour, accepted by most anthropologists, psychologists, and scientists, have a direct application to decision-makers.

1. Buyers, while usually having a main buying motive, are also swayed by subsidiary motives.
2. Buyers employed by different companies may buy the same product from the same supplier, but for different reasons.

Underlying Motives in Buying Decisions
One seller may have a price advantage, another an efficiency advantage, a third a design promotion scheme or packaging advantage over competitors, but each may lose orders by thinking in terms only of motivating a buyer because of the one potential advantage. While a buyer might appear to be mainly interested in design, he could also be motivated by security (e.g., heavy advertising, regular deliveries, a three-year guarantee). The sales agent having efficiency as his advantage might not appreciate that the buyer could be influenced in his decision through caution. And the seller who drives home the price advantage may not realise that the profit from repeat business which the customer is obtaining because of the ready demand for

a competitor's product motivates the buyer more than an immediate gain.

Each of these sales agents may well be able to cope with the buyer's need for security, fear, or increased profitability through repeat business, but overlook the need for emphasising these motives.

You may well now ask the questions:

> *But if people are motivated to act in different ways to reach a similar objective, how can I know which main motivator to use in my sales offer? Also, how do I discover subsidiary motivators?*

Regular calling will enable you to learn the motivators applying to individual buyers. You also learn by observation, by asking the buyer questions, and by listening to and assessing his replies. But you should include in your sales offer all the prime and subsidiary motivators applicable to your merchandise, product, or service. If a product or service has a different application for different buyers, it is feasible to use selective motivators.

> *The seller's objective must always be to try to include in his sales offer the motivational force or forces which will impel the buyer to buy.*

Buying Motives

A rational motive is one which is the result of reasoning: it stems from that part of the brain which is the powerhouse of rational thinking, the higher cortex. Emotion stems from a lower part of the brain; yet continually, the higher order of mental reasoning gives way to the lower order of emotional response. Over and over again, our emotions take precedence over reason.

Rationally, the late Edward, Duke of Windsor, should not have given up the throne of England to marry a divorced woman. However, emotionally, be could do no other than live with the woman he loved.

Rationally, a person should keep calm when faced with a situation which could lead to his dismissal at work. Emotionally, he might precipitate that dismissal by losing his temper.

What is all this about? you may ask. *Love of someone – losing a job – what help is that to a business-to-business seller?*

Recall this fact:

> *Every known action has a motive behind it – and all buyers, men and women, are human beings, with human frailties.*

When a managing director insists that a friend or client visit his office to see a new computer, his main objective is not to impress with the instant statistics of the computer. He shows his wares as a stamp collector shows his album. He is proud of his purchase – therefore, *pride* could have played a part when he placed his initial order for the computer.

Although it may be rare for sentiment to play a part in all forms of buying, it can apply. When a buyer purchases consumer goods from Bill Thomas & Son because she has done so for twenty-five years, it may be because these suppliers have always provided a fine service, but sentiment can play its part; otherwise, other suppliers would be tested out on occasion. A buyer will sometimes say, for example, 'I've seen that firm grow over twenty-five years, and I knew Bill Thomas very well.'

A seller should be aware of *sentiment* as a buying reason, if only to work out ways of overcoming it and getting his share of that buyer's business.

Emotional buying sometimes takes precedence during periods of strong nationalist feeling. When a sales agent says, 'We are a local firm and can give you quick service,' he is indirectly attempting to motivate a buyer by a *sentimental* appeal. No seller should ever say, 'You ought to buy from us because we are a local firm.' That is not playing on sentiment, but on charity.

One of the strongest of all emotional appeals is *the approval of others*. That pat on the back can mean as much to the owner of a small shop as it does to a professional buyer a managing director. Every buyer delights in hearing:

> *I like the display.*
> *You bought well.*
> *That new fork-lift truck is first-class.*
> *What a difference the new racking has made.*
> *You're moving the goods off the shelves faster than any of our other branches.*

You were very wise to change to leasing.

The professional salesperson knows that, and again, emotion plays a part in motivating a buyer to buy. Some car manufacturers take full-page advertisements in newspapers to stress the safety factor of their automobiles. Heading such an advertisement might be a picture of a mother with her two children. The caption could read: *Three important reasons why you should consider buying a Xerxes People Carrier for your holiday.* The copy might begin: *If you have a family, you must put safety at the top of your list.* Half-way down the page, there could be a sub-caption: *And twenty-three reasons more*, with the twenty-three safety factors then listed.

Few readers would study them carefully, but every reader would get the message: *If I love my family, I must buy a Xerxes People Carrier.*

All the advertisement needed was to state the twenty-three safety factors, and that should have been sufficient to motivate many potential buyers motivated by rational reasons. But its main appeal would really be an emotional one.

Classification of Buying Motives
- to gain or save money
- to satisfy caution
- to benefit health
- for protection and security
- its utility value
- to satisfy pride
- for pleasure
- for sentimental reasons
- fear
- envy
- for approval from others
- to prove social achievement
- to feel important

Here is a more specific classification of rational motives that are applicable to most salespeople:

Profit   direct gain of money – return from investment – cost reduction – increased output – less absenteeism – quicker selling lines

Efficiency	overall performance – it is faster – easier to handle – less risk of breakdown – less complicated – more powerful – quieter in operation – works to finer limits
Protection and Security	confidence in supplier – guaranteed standards – guaranteed deliveries – elimination of risk to employees – good after-sales service – wards off competition – heavily backed by advertising
Appearance	good design – compact – modern in its concept – wide colour range – appealing packaging
Durability	long life – less maintenance – withstands rough usage – less risk of breakdowns – customer satisfaction
Utility	time efficient – labour – effort – more convenient to use – easier to handle
Health	better working conditions – reduces strain – better environment – benefit to employees (cafeteria, food, air conditioning, lighting, etc.)

Because of his understanding of buyers' motivation, a salesperson is able to build a strong sales offer – one which will appeal to the widest range of buyers.

Problem-solving Motivators

When a buyer has a problem, he has worries, and no one likes worries. When a seller is told of a problem, he should give high priority to his customers' interests – provided that he knows the advice he may give will be within his company's policy.

When a buyer receives a stream of complaints because a component part keeps breaking down, he is a worried man. If his own Research and Development department cannot solve the problem, he probably lies awake at night thinking about it. When the experts try test after test, yet breakdowns still occur, it can be with real relief that he hears from a salesperson that his company might be able to help.

This may seem unusual in industry, but it happens time and time again. If that sales agent solves the problem, he is IN. He has given the buyer PROTECTION and SECURITY. He has also benefited the buyer's HEALTH. That buyer, in the future, will always give the seller a warm welcome and orders if possible.

When the managing director complains bitterly of rising costs, or shows his concern at low output, he will listen intently to the sales agent who can help to solve his problem.

It could be that a new machine is required, but, because of its size, a new factory layout would be needed. The seller of the machine could, perhaps, help to solve the layout problem as well (Motivation: PROFIT).

Or it might be that delivery costs are getting out-of-hand, which could be solved by a well-qualified salesperson selling a specialised delivery service. Perhaps there is a cash problem – liquidity. The agent who is selling a leasing service – equipment, plant, cars – could help solve this problem by proving how capital can be used more efficiently (Motivation: EFFICIENCY).

All sales agents must remind themselves continually that a prime motivator is helping a buyer to solve problems. There are other quite dissimilar problems which buyers have to deal with, and which salespeople can help them to resolve.

The professional seller knows that he is not only in direct competition with competitors, but also with the day-to-day demands made upon buyer – demands from associates and employees.

No company, however large, can afford to buy everything offered to it: more luxurious offices – an in-house gym – a private executive aircraft – private health schemes – more sophisticated computers – bigger cars for sales staff . . . And no managing director can agree to all the demands made upon him by the various departments in his organisation.

A managing director has to withstand this type of pressure

continually. Research and development may want new testing equipment – the plant manager cannot do without new paint-spraying booths – the production manager must have that new, expensive, all-purpose piece of machinery – the dispatch manager wants more lorries, while the warehouse manager wants extra warehouse space – Public Relations, conscious of the company image, wants a landscape gardener to lay out the fields in front of the factory – the financial director needs highly sophisticated new financial software – and on the factory floor the cleaner wants new vacuums and the restaurant manager needs better dishwashers.

The salesperson calling on that company has to compete for the firm's cash. He has to make that managing director (or his buyer) give his product or service priority over the software, the garden landscaping, the paint-spraying booths, etc.

How, then, can a seller use his knowledge of motivators to persuade a buyer to give his product or service this priority?

The answer is: by creating a *want* in the mind of the buyer.

Creating Wants

There are specific areas in which a seller can create the right atmosphere for a buyer to *want* the merchandise, products or services he is offering. Even a specifying authority – architect, consulting engineer, welfare officer – will only make a decision when he wants to favour one supplier instead of another.

Understanding motivational forces allows a seller to create a desire to buy by appealing to a buyer's *wants*. And what we all *want* when we buy are benefits to ourselves, our families, or our company; and if we are retailers, then benefits to our customers. There is no one point in a sale when desire is created, any more than there is one time only when confidence is established. A seller is always building confidence in himself and his company – and every time he shows a buyer a benefit, he should be creating a *want*. The seller who builds benefit after benefit is the professional, who gets more than his share of the business.

While most minds are influenced by emotional motivators, all benefits are based on rational motivators.

Understanding motivational forces allows a salesperson to concentrate on the main benefits which appeal to a particular buyer:

Buyer A is mainly motivated by profitability.
Buyer B is mainly motivated by security.
Buyer C is mainly motivated by efficiency.

Salesperson Jones will show Buyer A the benefit of profitability to be derived from his product or service and will bring these benefits up (quick turnover – high demand) again and again; while Salesperson Brown, selling to Buyer B, will concentrate on proving the benefits of regular deliveries: a twenty-four-hour service – standards maintained. Salesperson White, selling to Buyer C, demonstrates that the efficiency of her product must benefit the buyer's production line.

The professional salesperson, while concentrating on the main benefits offered by his product or service, will, however, never overlook all the subsidiary benefits. It is often these subsidiary benefits which will finally motivate a buyer to buy.

Salespeople also create *wants* by talking in terms of what a product *does* rather than what it *is*.

Do you buy a duvet because the salesperson tells you that the insulation value of the polyester filling is such and such, or do you buy because the professional salesperson has told you: 'With this duvet you will feel extra warm in the winter and cool in the summer'?

Does a buyer buy because the seller, steeped in technicalities, says, 'This melamine-formaldehyde resin, when used in admixture with alkyd resins, gives a much faster heat cure than when a urea-formaldehyde resin is used alone. The outstanding characteristics which urea resins supply to films are further enhanced with melamine resins, which are then resistant to various chemical re-agents and maintain durability and colour retention to heat and light'?

Or does he buy because the professional seller has said, 'The melamine–formaldehyde resin is used with alkyd resins, so that you will be able to produce a porcelain-like appearance resistant to abrasions and heat'?

Does a buyer buy because a salesperson says, 'Our new pack is made of double strength *Riebelene* and to open it you only have to press a small plastic button'? Or does he buy because the salesperson says, '*Your* customers will keep coming back for more, because the *Riebelene* pack means a negligible risk of spillage – no more mopping up – and the new spout makes the package much easier to open, too.

Buyers buy for the latter reasons – those given by professional sales agents who always translate technicalities into direct benefits to the buyer or company.

Motivation by Filling Needs and Stimulating Wants

In every industry, there are basic needs catered for by a host of suppliers – raw materials, component parts, standard tools, packaging supplies, every kind of merchandise, consumer goods and consumer durables. These needs could be counted by the hundreds in some factories, by the thousands in others, by the dozens in shops and stores. Suppliers of basic needs are usually in a highly competitive market. Every week a buyer will see sales-people eager to tell him why he should buy from them, instead of from his current suppliers, disinfectants or ball bearings, cleaning materials or switchgear, overalls for staff or electric motors, soaps or detergents, dresses and coats . . .

What motivates a buyer to change suppliers or agree to a change in the specification of the product he is buying regularly from one of his suppliers? He will only change his mind if there will be additional benefits from switching to a new supplier or agreeing to changes in specification.

To change the mind of a buyer, a seller must, therefore, turn a basic need into a *want* – a *want* for his product or service. As the main buying benefit is usually already obtainable from the present supplier, the salesperson who is competing to fill a basic need must be sure of selling every subsidiary benefit offered by his product. One of these could be the motivator to change a basic need into a *want* for his product.

Unrecognised or True Needs

An *unrecognised need*, usually referred to as the *true need*, is sometimes obvious, sometimes not. For example, before domestic refrigerators were on the market, although block ice was often used to keep food cool, in the majority of households food was kept in cellars or food safes, or was stood in bowls of water. As far as the people of those times were concerned, their need was being filled. The food was just that shade cooler, lasted just that little bit longer than if it were left in an outside, warmer atmosphere, so these simple methods filled the need. When, eventually, household refrigerators were marketed, which filled the *true need*, there was a great deal of resistance to buying. Housewives believed that except perhaps in very hot weather, they had no food deterioration problems, and were content with their food safes, etc. Salespeople who sold refrigerators then had a very difficult job persuading people to *want* a refrigerator, because the housewives did not recognise their *true need*.

The recognising of *true needs* is not confined to the householder; skilled buyers, brilliant managing directors, heads of production units, etc., often do not recognise their *true needs*. Photocopiers are now looked upon as essential office equipment – yet when they were first launched on the market they met with extreme resistance. It was not until sales agents were able to *create want* by showing the *true need* that photocopying made headway. Nowadays, salespeople have to find those *extra benefits* to enable them to compete with the market leaders.

Directors used to believe that true needs could be satisfied by massive filing systems – which grew over the years, entailing the use of many filing cabinets and causing overcrowding in offices. But their *true needs* were for information storage and retrieval systems which were satisfied by computer networks. These *needs* being unrecognised, early sellers of computer systems had to emphasise their benefits – until the *want* was created.

Often, in the retail trade, there is an unrecognised need for better quality and higher-priced products, but the retailer is obsessed with the belief that in his district no one will pay the higher price of the quality goods.

Retailers and wholesalers often have to be persuaded that they do not need more of X at £100 plus, but should stock Y at £100 plus, and create new business for themselves.

Here is an example from Nu-aire, a company within our own group, which saw that a whole dimension in building design could be opened up if a certain product were made available. The building industry did not, at first, recognise the *need*.

British building regulations state that a toilet/bathroom must either be provided with a window which can be opened or with a mechanical extractor system which changes the air in the room a specified number of times in the hour. Also, various local recommendations specify that the fan system serving these internal rooms must be of the standby type, so that, should the fan fail, the reserve fan automatically takes over.

All these rules are designed to protect the health of tenants and are strictly enforced by both the public health inspector and the building inspectorate.

For many years, the need for ventilation had been met by special fans designed to serve internal bathrooms. They were limited to sizes suitable for a number of rooms linked together by a common duct system, and therefore the only occasions on which internal bathrooms were used were in fairly high-rise buildings. Because of this situation, low- and medium-rise buildings were not designed with internal bathrooms. On the other hand, there were quite obvious pressures on the building industry to bring these rooms into the internal core of the construction. These reasons were:

1. Lack of suitable building land and its cost made narrow-frontage dwellings attractive to the developers and architects.
2. The grouping together of all services in the central core reduced costs.

Nu-Aire recognised a *need*, and designed a range of small units suitable for ventilating individual internal bathrooms. They satisfied the various standards, were inexpensive, and most important, they could be selected and detailed by the architect without help from specialised service engineers.

After the *true need* was explained by Nu-aire salespeople, the demand was created. These units subsequently directly influenced architecture in this country, so that, today, internal bathrooms are a feature of dwellings, from low- to high-rise types. However, in spite of the uniqueness of these units, Nu-aire sales agents, time and time again, had to make the *need* for the units recognised, and then *create the want*.

BUYER MOTIVATION

To summarise, here are the steps to an appreciation of buyer motivation:

1. There is a motive behind every human action.
2. There is always a prime motive and a subsidiary motive. The seller, while concentrating on the prime motive, must never overlook the subsidiary motives.
3. Different buyers buy similar equipment, but often for different reasons. Selective motives should be used when applicable.
4. There are rational and emotional buying motives, and the importance of emotional motives must never be underrated.
5. The seller's objective must always be to try to include in his sales offer the motivational force or forces which will impel the buyer to buy.
6. Buyers first fulfil *true needs*, but often do not *recognise* their *true needs*.
7. Benefits should be 'personalised'.
8. A salesperson turns *needs* into *wants* by proving benefits to the buyer or company.

BENEFITS

Understanding buyer motivation means appreciating why and how he arrives at his decisions – why a buyer has a fear of change. And, most important, it enables a seller to *progress an interview*. This means that, while he is actually selling, he will know – not by intuition but by sheer logic – how a buyer will react to claims, statements and offers ... and the underlying thoughts of the buyer when objections are raised.

> *The professional salesperson also knows that it is benefits derived from a knowledge of buyer motivation which act as a stimulus, and develop a want in the mind of the buyer.*

7

Obtaining the Interview

It is wise to be armed with every scrap of information that can help you to close an order. It is right to plan your sales offer. It is correct to check your sales kit before a call. But these preparations are wasted if a prospective buyer won't see you. Interviews can be hard to get when a buyer is well guarded.

Managing directors, production managers, project managers, purchasing personnel advertising managers, store buyers, buyers for retail chains, are usually in their offices or workshops, and between them and the salesperson are assistants, PAs, receptionists, and other staff – all ready to bar the way.

Whether a seller is seen by a buyer largely depends on his need for the product or service being offered. Salespeople selling repeat products, and to many retail outlets, have no problems getting interviews. But salespeople selling capital goods, services, or trying to open new accounts for component parts or any form of merchandise often waste valuable time getting appointments to be seen, when they should be spending their time selling.

Appointments by Telephone

How can a seller get the maximum number of interviews? What are his alternatives? He can call cold, or make an appointment by telephone or mail plus follow-up through a telephone appointment agency.

Even if he is given inquiries to follow up, he will, more often than not, have to telephone for an appointment. Cold calling or prospecting, as it is sometimes termed, will always have its place in selling, but it is usually a fill-in for most salespeople. Rather than waste time between appointments a seller will often call cold on any near-by prospects, but prospecting as a planned system of working can be very time-consuming. For example, there can be long waits in reception areas until the buyer is disengaged. Also, a full day's work may result in only two good interviews. But telephoning in advance may enable a seller to make four or five appointments a day.

Preparation

Unless the telephone call is made on a routine basis by a seller calling on his customers every few weeks or months, and these customers like to set aside time to see him, the basis of all telephone selling – and making appointments by telephone is hard selling – must be good preparation. There are several rules to follow before making an appointment by telephone to prospective buyers, and one golden rule:

You must find out the prospect's name and get it right.

Knowing the prospect's name will help you to handle the receptionist, and by addressing the buyer by name you are able to bring immediate warmth to the relationship.

When you telephone either customer or prospect, remember:

1. You must have customer files or databases available. This information allows you to anticipate a customer's or prospect's questions or objections to giving an interview. A customer may have had a delivery complaint. A prospect might not have purchased from you previously because he considered your prices too high. With this knowledge available you can forestall his queries.
2. Websites, directories, brochures, and any other information which you may need should be to hand. The names and telephone numbers of calls you intend making should be in front of you, and of course a means of making notes.
3. Your diary is invaluable to you. Whenever possible you will suggest days and times for appointments to suit *your* convenience. Your aim must be to fill the day with appointments.
4. Make sure that you will not be disturbed while telephoning.
5. It is always better to dial yourself if you can. It is never as good if someone else phones on your behalf, although it can be more economical for your company in the short-term.

Now, are you ready? Let us assume that your name is White, and that you are calling a production director called Ms Smith. Although you want to speak to Ms Smith personally, you must *never* make a misleading statement to obtain your objectives.

Making a Call
Pick up the telephone, dial the number, and on being greeted by the receptionist, ask to speak to Ms Smith.

One of three things can happen:

1. The receptionist will transfer you immediately to Ms Smith, and all will be well.
2. The receptionist will ask you your business.
3. The receptionist may put you through to Ms Smith's secretary.

To avoid 2 and 3, you must have an authoritative approach:

'Will you please tell Ms Smith, your production manager, that John White is on the line. Thank you.'

The *John* personalises the approach. Never use a prefix like Mr or Ms for your own name. The *thank you* gives it a finality which does not invite any response. Unless the receptionist has special screening instructions regarding incoming calls, you will be put through to Ms Smith.

Now we come to 2. The receptionist asks you for further information. You answer quite simply:

'It is a business matter.'

Don't add anything further. It is not a misleading statement because it is a business matter (not a personal call) which you can discuss only with the production manager.

Alternatively, it will show equal authority if you imply that you wish to discuss something of importance – for example:

'It is in connection with Ms Smith's new factory production plans – output – forecast . . .'

There is another excellent approach if a letter has been sent in advance to the buyer. Then you can say,

> 'It is with reference to the letter I wrote . . .'

If the receptionist has been instructed to insist on obtaining information from every caller asking for Ms Smith, you must say,

> 'I am sorry but it is a very involved matter. I think it might be best if you put me through to Ms Smith's PA.'

It is sometimes advisable when making appointments to ask for a PA in the first place, but in the main it is better to ask the executive concerned. The PA may be away from the office, and in this event the receptionist *may* put you straight through to the person you want to contact.

If you do speak to the PA, however, either by your own request or because the receptionist has instructions, you will then have the selling task of persuading her to make an appointment for you to see Ms Smith.

You will use the golden words:

> '*I should like to ask your advice.* I want to see Ms Smith because . . .'

You will not win every time, but you will win far more often than you will lose. In the majority of cases you will, therefore, be able to speak to Ms Smith.

What do you say?

The Hook

There should, whenever possible, be a hook on which to hang your approach. This can be a letter which you or your company have written, an advertisement, a new product – special claim you can make for your product – or a reference from a friend or business associate.

Your approach could be:

> 'Ms Smith, this is John White of the Bridgwater Machine Tool Company. Have you a moment to speak on the telephone?'

This courteous request – 'Have you a moment . . .' – is not laid down as a fixed rule. It can, however, be very effective. It relaxes the prospect because you have only asked her for a moment of her time. Also, it shows a courtesy that is lacking in so many telephone calls.

Whether you use this sentence or not, you must now repeat the prospect's name, after you have given her the name of your company.

Letter Hook

'Ms Smith, did you receive my letter?'
'No, what was it about?'
'Ms Smith, it was about your . . .'

Reference Hook

'Ms Smith, we haven't met, but Joan Williams asked me to contact you . . .'

You then have to sell Ms Smith the idea that you are worth seeing.

Question Hook
When you haven't a hook of any kind, ask a question:

'Ms Smith, this is Mike Boon of the Bessing Group. Have you heard of our organisation?'

Whether you receive the reply 'Yes' or 'No' is immaterial, because it will take you smoothly into the main reason for your call.

The Quick Approach Close
In all forms of selling, it is axiomatic that a seller should think of the close the minute the sale begins, but in telephone selling there is a difference. You can actually close at the approach.

The buyer might be influenced by the name of your company, or interested in the product or service you are selling, or like the sound of your voice – you sound like someone she should listen to – or it may even be that she is very busy and arrives at a quick decision. Whatever the reason, this form of approach does get appointments. This is how to do it:

With conviction in your voice, to create the impression that there cannot be a refusal, you say,

> 'Good morning Mr Jones, this is Jack Smith of Halliday Publications. I should like to take up just eight minutes of your time to tell you about our new journal for your industry and its wonderful advertising pull. Would Wednesday morning or Wednesday afternoon be more convenient for me to call?'

This approach covers a lot of ground. It is brief; it asks for only a short interview; it states your business; it closes.

Be Special

A wonderful word to use in all approaches is *special*, or *specially*:

> 'Mr Jones, I am calling you *specially* to tell you about . . .'
> 'Ms Smith, there is a *special* reason why I should like to see you . . .'

Keep to the Rules

Although the quick close will get you interviews, in many cases there will be a request for further information.

Here are some points to remember:

- Time is not on your side, so keep the benefit short.
- You must not become involved in a full sales offer.
- Keep the objective in mind: *to obtain an interview*.
- Use short sentences.
- Use understandable words.
- Be authoritative, but never talk down to the buyer.
- Do not try to be too clever. You have to persuade the prospect that you are a sincere person by the words you use, and by the tone of your voice.
- You must have a reason for not giving full information over the telephone, e.g., samples to be shown, a model of a

building to examine, figures to analyse, a drawing to discuss, or matters so personal that they should be discussed face-to-face.

The Main Benefit

You must stake your claim for an interview in a few compelling words:

'I'd like to show you some recent information on . . .'

'You will want to consider six ideas for cutting down overheads in your offices . . .'

'We have designed a very unusual savings plan which will be of great benefit to you . . .'

'This new personal computer is no bigger than your writing pad. Knowing something of your company's activities, I'm sure you would find this of tremendous help for personal use . . .'

'You will want to handle the stitcher yourself; to see how well it works . . .'

Your aim is to intrigue the prospect, to interest him so that he will want to hear more and will give you an interview.

The Objections

What could be his objections? He can hardly object to your product or service, because you have only given him the barest outline. He could only object to you taking up his time at an interview.

He could answer:

'I will see you' – and all will be well.
'Send me the information.'
'Tell me now.'
'I'm too busy.'

There are several ways of tackling a request for further information

'Mr Smith, you will want to see proof of how a company

has been able to increase overall production by up to 28 per cent.'

'What I want to talk to you about, Mr Brown, is details of a new way in which you can protect your money and beat inflation. Would next Tuesday morning . . .?'

'Mrs Jones, you demand a very fast delivery service. We can provide that at low cost, and you will want to examine this claim. It is for this reason that I want the opportunity of meeting you. May I call . . .'

'I cannot advise you, Mr Black, until I know one or two things about your company . . .'

'You would need to look at our analysis forms, Ms Clark, and I'll bring them with me. It will only take a few minutes. May I call on . . .?'

To the statement, 'I am too busy', the salesperson has several answers, according to what he is selling.

'That is why I am telephoning you, Mr Smith, because I know you are so busy. I can help you in this direction by cutting down some of the demands on your time.'

Ego building can also be a sound policy:

'Ms White, I have found that it is the busy people like you who are most interested . . .'

Or assume that the prospect is only encountering a temporary rush of business:

'Of course, Mr Howell, I know how busy you are. I was not thinking of disturbing you today or tomorrow. Will you be able to see me on Thursday or Friday of next week?'

If you reach a point where you feel you are antagonising the prospect, then you must never shut the door to a future appointment.

'I'll call you again in a fortnight's time, Mr Smith.'

If this does not work, there is always one final request which you can make. It is rarely refused:

'Mr Smith, there are some times of the day when you are
not so busy as others – although I appreciate that you
cannot specify them. When I am near your offices, may I
call on the off-chance of seeing you?'

He will nearly always say 'Yes' and this is noted in your cold-
calling diary.

Following the telephone call, after two or three visits at the
most, you will find that you will see Mr Smith.

The Close

Tying up an appointment is different from locking up an order,
when you can use any of the closes set out in the sales
presentation. This is not possible when selling the interview.
Nearly always, therefore, you will use the *Alternative Close*, based
on an appointment time.

Most sales agents suggest a time for a meeting on the hour or
the half-hour. You can be different. Put forward 9.10 a.m. or 3.50
p.m., or very early or late if this suits the buyer.

The very unexpected nature of this suggestion will often bring
its own reward, but the main reason for using this technique is
that many busy people make appointments on the hour or half-
hour, some of which will last for the full period, while others will
be cut short. The odd time, therefore, will often appeal to the
prospect whose appointments on the hour may leave him periods
in between which are free.

Remember, you are only asking for a few minutes of his time,
knowing that if you interest him he will ask you to stay. The close
can, therefore, be:

> 'Will Wednesday or Thursday suit you best, Mrs Lovell?'
> 'Er – Wednesday.'
> 'Morning, or afternoon?'
> 'Afternoon is best for me.'
> 'That's fine, Mrs Lovell, can you make it two-ten? Or
> would four-fifty be more convenient?'
> 'Ten past two would suit me.'

'Thank you, Mrs Lovell, I'll look forward to being with you at ten past two on Wednesday.'

Example:
(The sales agent of Arrow Weighing is telephoning a director seeking an appointment.)

'Mr Harvey? Good morning, this is Peter Lisle of Arrow Weighing. We met some three years ago when the maintenance contract on your equipment was arranged. Can you spare me a moment?'

'Yes.'

'Mr Harvey, the contract is due for renewal next month. You will want to see the new proposal – may I call on Wednesday . . .?'

'There's no need for you to come here – you can post the papers on to me.'

'Thank you, Mr Harvey. But reports from my engineers show that certain machines are being used either less or more than they were three years ago. You will agree that we should try to get the frequency of maintenance on each machine in relation to its use and importance. On Wednesday, I can explain . . .'

'You'd better talk to my chief engineer about this – he'll know what he wants and I will accept his recommendations, provided the charge for the contract isn't any higher than before. Costs seem to keep rising.'

'They do indeed, Mr Harvey, and you will understand that in providing a service a very high proportion of the premium is directly related to labour costs – and we both know how salaries keep going up. In any event, you and I can work this out between us, and I'm sure you will agree that we should have a talk about it. Would Wednesday . . . ?'

Particular Points

1. Reason for call made clear. Mr Harvey might have agreed to

see the sales agent without more discussion.

2. A valid, although secondary reason for wanting an appointment.

3. The primary reason comes out but is not dealt with, as Peter Lisle does not want to become involved in a price discussion. The need for the meeting is brought to a 'you and I' situation. Lisle has raised the importance of the issue, and has built up Mr Harvey's ego.

Conclusion

To succeed in obtaining more appointments by telephone, you must:

- know your prospects and their business
- have a definite reason for asking for the interview
- have a planned approach
- have a main benefit to stress the need for the appointment
- be prepared to listen, and don't pounce (It might be that the prospect is about to give you an interview when you interrupt.)
- smile when you talk on the telephone
- talk a little slower than usual
- if not making headway, ask questions
- sound enthusiastic (Your enthusiasm will be transmitted and will do more than anything else to get that appointment for you.)

The obtaining of appointments is a challenge to all salespeople – a challenge which, if accepted, can lead to a greater volume of business.

Prospecting

Visiting cards have their uses when calling on customers. A buyer who sees many sales agents cannot be expected to remember every name, but if he has the visiting card before him, sent in by the receptionist, he can refresh his mind by glancing at it. Sometimes a buyer asks for a card. Rather than apologise for not having one, carry a card. Also, if you can get an appointment by sending through your card, then keep a good supply readily available. But if you have frequently called on a buyer, each time sending up your card, and each time failing in your mission, you must work according to a different plan.

The card might show the name of a company – Johnsons Tools, for example. A buyer glances at it, and being satisfied with his present suppliers, returns it with the message: *nothing today*. But the agent representing Johnsons Tools might have a special tool which would interest that buyer; this information cannot be learned from the card.

Thousands of salespeople make thousands of abortive calls, because they persist in using cards for the wrong reasons. Following is a technique which usually brings about interviews.

If a reception office is 'guarded' by a receptionist, it is essential that you walk briskly up to the reception desk. If you have a hangdog look or appear ill-at-ease, you won't succeed even in the first part of your task, which is to convey a sense of the importance of your visit to the receptionist.

You smile and say, 'Good morning, will you please tell Mr Brown that Tim Heyworth is here to see him.'

If you indicate that you expect to be questioned by her, she will invariably, ask, 'What is your business?' In most cases, she will telephone Mr Brown and tell him that Mr Tim Heyworth is in the waiting-room to see him. Mr Brown then has two choices: he can ask the receptionist, 'Will you please find out what he wants,' or he can say, 'Tell him to come up and see me.'

If, however, the receptionist asks for information, you must give it. If, when telephoning Mr Brown, she says, 'Mr Brown has asked the reason for your visit,' try to answer Mr Brown's question yourself. You need only say, 'May I just have a word with him?' Now it is up to you to convince Mr Brown that he should see you.

This technique, therefore, gives an opportunity for an interview which is impossible when you use a card. Success is not guaranteed but the method is well worth trying – even today.

Here are rules to remember for obtaining more interviews:

1. Treat receptionists with respect to obtain their co-operation.
2. Don't wait about too long. Your time is valuable. If someone is going to keep you waiting thirty or forty minutes, it may pay you better to make a call elsewhere.
3. If there is any reading matter relating to the firm's activities in the reception office, study it while you are waiting.
4. If you are kept waiting a little while, don't keep pestering the receptionist.
5. When a secretary comes into the waiting-room, don't forget to stand up, and she will appreciate words like, 'I should be grateful for your help', or, 'I wonder if you can help me . . .' Most people like to help others.

8

Pre-planning

Here are some scenes of a seller in action:

Scene I. A Production Manager's Office

PRODUCTION MANAGER: The idea seems good, but it won't be easy to incorporate it in our system. Have you a drawing?

SELLER *(delving into his bag):* Yes, of course. Here it is – no, it isn't, this is the one *(taking a crumpled piece of paper out of his bag).* Sorry, that's a drawing of the larger unit. *(He rummages again, muttering.)* I know it's here somewhere – I was only using it an hour ago. Ah, this should be it . . .

Couldn't happen? Doesn't happen? It occurs over and over again.

Pre-planning means that every sample – every sales aid – every brochure – must be packed so neatly that a seller can extract any piece he requires without taking his eyes away from the customer.

Scene II. A Receptionist's Office

RECEPTIONIST: May I help you?

SELLER: I would like to see the person who buys office supplies, please.

RECEPTIONIST: We have several executives – they purchase for their own departments.

SELLER: Well, I need to see the one who buys printer cartridges.

RECEPTIONIST: That would be our general manager. I'm sorry, she only sees representatives by appointment.

SELLER: Okay, I'll write then.

Couldn't happen? It did – to us.

Pre-planning means finding out the name of the correct buyer before the call.

Scene III. A Retail Shop

SELLER: Good morning, Miss Jones. I have just got a repeat order for the dresses that have been selling so well. I persuaded Mr Smith to put in an extra order for ones in canary – it's a new colour. They should sell well, don't you think?

Ms Jones looks annoyed and turns away. Later:

SELLER: What's the matter with Miss Jones this morning?
SECOND ASSISTANT: You called her Miss Jones. She told you last time you were here that she's Ms Jones – and she also told you that the new canary shade doesn't sell well for us.

Pre-planning means using a database system of some kind. Salespeople of consumer goods are so sure they know everything about their regular customers that they feel there is no need to keep such records. But salespeople often make mistakes – especially in human relations – because they have bad memories. The help that can be given by an assistant like Ms Jones has been mentioned. Buyers always listen to members of their staff. Managing directors are swayed by their PAs, and production managers by shop foremen. Up-to-date records should be kept with the names of assistants, their special preferences, whether they are married or single, when they take holidays, and so on.

Scene IV. An Accountant's Office

SELLER: Good morning, Ms Smith, I wanted to talk to you about the inquiry you sent us.
ACCOUNTANT: I've told you several times not to call during the first week of the month while we are doing our accounts; it is most inconvenient, as we are doing the accounts for last month. You should have telephoned for an appointment.

Pre-planning means finding the best time to call. This may not apply to speciality agents or those selling consumer goods, but it does apply to most representatives selling capital equipment.

Scene V. A Pub

SELLER: Spurs are in great form – they'll walk all over Leeds on Saturday.

PUBLICAN: Now that's where you're wrong. You don't know what football's about. As I was born in Yorkshire, I've followed Leeds for . . .

Pre-planning means learning something of a prospect's background. The salesperson deduced that the publican must be a Spurs supporter because his premises were on the Spurs' home grounds. If he was not sure of his facts, he should have avoided discussing football.

Scene VI. An Office

SELLER: Well, that's the whole proposition. I'm glad you are so interested, and I'm sure you'd like to tie everything up now. I'll just write down the details.

OFFICE MANAGER: No, don't do that! You will remember I told you I can't actually sign orders. You'll have to see our director.

Pre-planning means finding out as much as possible about a company's personnel and the authority of each executive to place orders. Is the company a limited liability company, or is it a partnership? If the latter, does one partner have the right to buy without consulting the other? If a manufacturer, does he make quality or cheap products? How many employees? What is the firm's credit rating?

The more information a sales agent can gather, the more success he will have in turning a prospect into a customer.

OBTAINING INFORMATION

There is a mine of information awaiting the seller who will trouble to dig for it.

Call Centres
Many of your prospects will now have call centres – usually with

free numbers. Try calling in for information, like one of their potential clients would.

Websites
Most businesses (even small ones) now have good websites. Always start there – usually the information is extensive and regularly updated.

Head Office
What do your company's top executives know of a customer? Sometimes they have a great deal of information, but they do not give it to the sales team without being asked. Ask!

Local Traders
The speciality seller making anything from ten to twenty calls a day cannot check prospective customers with head office. But local traders will often talk about their neighbours. Even if a seller is unsuccessful at a call, he can still ask for information. He may ask:

> 'Can you tell me the name of the practice manager of the solicitors' firm opposite?'
> 'Has she been there long?'
> 'What kind of a person is she?'
> 'Is she a partner?

The answers will help him make a good approach to that firm of solicitors.

Newspapers
Salespeople should read more newspapers. A representative selling high-priced equipment should read the city pages. He will learn of new developments, of the background of top executives, and new plans for expansion. In company reports he will find further information to help him talk in terms of the customer's interests.

The salesperson selling to smaller traders should get local newspapers. There may be nothing useful in them for 25 weeks

out of 26, but on the twenty-sixth week there may be something that will indicate a sales opportunity at a local factory or local government office.

A shop owner is always pleased when a representative mentions his advertisement in the *Watling Gazette*, or what the editor of the *Blankton Star* wrote of his special window display, or a reference to his speech at the opening of an old people's home.

Some sales agents do better than others because they take their jobs more seriously. It is time-consuming to read local newspapers, but such time spent in preparation for an order is always worthwhile.

Trade magazines can also keep sales staff up-to-date in many aspects of their job. Public companies increase in size, with City Editors ready to pounce at the least sign of inefficiency or a fall in profits. The people who get to the top give that little bit extra – extra study of a project, extra homework, extra thought to a sales drive, extra care with a new production programme, extra courage, extra effort to sell abroad, and so on. Most people don't want to sacrifice their time to 'extras'. They want success without effort.

Directories and Databases

New directories and databases seem to be launched on the Internet, on CD and in printed form every week. At most firms, details of new databases with up-to-date information about companies and company directors are received regularly. No company could be expected to buy all of these databases, but they are nearly always available at local libraries or through trade associations or professional bodies. In directories, you can find:

- names of directors of companies
- scholastic background of directors
- names and address of companies within a group
- products manufactured or sold by a division of an organisation
- capital structure
- number of employees.

Observation

Good observation plays a part in pre-planning. A change of name on a board in a multi-company office, or a good window display, can help a salesperson surmount the first hurdle of the approach. The store buyer's preferences may be seen in the range of goods in the windows. It might be too late to obtain a contract when it is seen that a site is being levelled for a new building, but there could still be opportunities with the building director or developer. The seller can learn something from the types of cars parked outside offices, the decor of a waiting room, the letter-heading of a company's notepaper, advertising campaigns, the general staff atmosphere.

Other Salespeople

Salespeople are, by nature, talkative. Analytical chemists or accountants do not talk a great deal about their work, but salespeople are always ready to describe victories or defeats. Listeners, we know, can always learn something and other salespeople can be surprisingly helpful. Many a useful hint has been picked up from their idle chatter at the end of the day.

They will refer to the peculiarities of customers, the ease with which a receptionist can be out-manoeuvred, the new machinery being installed in a certain factory, a new shop being opened . . .

No honourable salesperson would get information from a competitor who might be ignorant of his reason for asking, but representatives selling non-competitive goods have much to teach. A salesperson selling office machinery may have noticed that new partitioning is needed. A book seller may know of a new store's department for cosmetics.

Make friends with other salespeople – they can be good friends to you.

The Pre-Planning Data Sheet

Your pre-planning inquiries should be recorded on your database. For instance, a sales agent of fire extinguishers may assemble all the facts likely to help him at a factory, and his screen could read:

Name of Company:	Jones Motors Ltd
Address:	Meadowland, Kent, TN27 3BE
E-mail	info@jonesmotorskent.com
Website	www.jonesmotors.co.uk
Telephone no:	01789 12345
Associate companies:	Boon & Boon Ltd, Topworth, Essex
Authority to buy:	Managing Director, F. D. Jones
Influence in buying:	Partner, S. R. Smith
Employees:	Kent, about 150; in Essex, 130
Present system:	Units installed about twelve years ago. Cannot find out name of manufacturer. It seems that service is given irregularly.
Fire hazards:	The usual, but special risk in warehouse where employees are allowed to smoke. Cigarette ends seen on floor. Should be influenced by fire recently at nearby mill.
Buying authority:	Man. Dir. Chairman of local Conservative Association. Played cricket for local team. Anti-blood-sports. Has son in business in Accounts Dept. (Accounts Dept on top floor – fire risk.) Married, but now widower. Self-made man and proud of it.
	Smith has been with company 20 years. Loyal. Thinks very little of salespeople. Likes facts. Member of local Dramatic Society.
Other details:	Must see Man. Dir. but will see Prod. Man. and tell him of appointment with Man. Dir. Must get his interest in first place.
	Must get large order or nothing. Co. may shortly seek stock exchange quotation. What would happen if fire before then?

The bigger the potential business, the more time and trouble is justified. But all prospects deserve some time investment.

The Planners
Salespeople can be placed roughly (very roughly) in three categories:

- the meticulous planner
- the constant planner
- the semi-planner.

Even the most unprofessional seller will do some pre-call planning, if it is only giving thought to the name of the buyer, or where he should park his car.

The *meticulous planner*, however, plans carefully each evening, firstly completing his report, then entering its details onto a database. Next he considers his work for the following day – what time should he spend telephoning to get appointments? Or if his appointments are already made, how long should he spend with each buyer? What are their needs? And so on . . .

The *constant planner* is nearly always an enthusiast, deeply concerned with every aspect of his job. He is continually planning thinking ahead. When the late Ian Fleming was asked, 'When do you plan the writing of a book?' he answered, 'All the time!' This statement is true of most authors. They are always delving into their minds to solve problems, to think of improvements for the next chapter, to re-plan a chapter already written, to consider the best approach to a publisher, to weigh up the film rights . . .

These thoughts pass through their minds while driving, taking the dog for a walk, pretending to listen to the tittle-tattle of cocktail parties . . .

The author is no different from the seller who is a *constant planner* – except for report-writing, the latter does not necessarily set aside a special time for planing, because he is always planning – always jotting down notes.

Unfortunately, many a seller is a *semi-planner*, believing that he can *play it by ear*. He doesn't bother to keep even a proper manual record system, relying on his memory to retrieve details of customers' requirements, names of decision influencers, etc.

An example of the difference between the *meticulous planner* and the *semi-planner* is that the first will always carry coins with him for use in a parking meter. The *semi-planner* would never dream of checking whether he had the coins in his pocket each morning, and sometimes has to make this excuse to a customer: 'I'm so sorry I'm late, but I didn't have a coin for the meter. Believe it or not, I couldn't find a single passer-by who had change.'

The *semi-planner* is a muddler, who only does well if he is an outstandingly good seller.

There are three stages in planning:

1. At regular intervals throughout the year.
2. Once a week.
3. Daily.

PLANNING AT REGULAR INTERVALS THROUGHOUT THE YEAR

Business is ever-changing; facts – information – given to a seller are altered regularly. This necessitates a continual reassessment of:

- product knowledge
- competitors and their products.

A seller must also remind himself of the special features of his product or service at least once a month. Familiarity with a product can lead to a mental blockage, or mental laziness. If these mental aberrations are not checked, orders can be lost.

A buyer on the friendliest of terms with a seller may say:

'I didn't know you *also* supplied hoses – I've given the order to . . .'

Buyers often buy from competitors because they don't know the full extent of the range of equipment of a trusted and regular supplier. A buyer is also apt to forget special features, and unless reminded of them will say, for example:

'I didn't know your units could be adapted to a central system – I thought you only made them for individual use. I've given the order to . . .'

If a salesperson doesn't remind himself constantly of these features which helped him to get the order initially, he can lose repeat business. Reminders are an essential part of preparation.

WEEKLY PLANNING

A name sometimes given to weekly planning is *armchair planning*. This conjures up visions of the seller at home, seated in an armchair, the children having been warned off, deep in thought, with mind acutely alert, thinking ahead, planning the close of a sale.

A very nice, comforting picture, but most sellers would find it extremely difficult to arrange to have that kind of peace on a Saturday or Sunday. All *armchair planning* really means is taking 'time off' to deliberate and work out strategies for the week ahead. Maybe this does take place when the family have gone to bed, or before embarking on a Sunday morning walk. Somehow, time has to be found, unless you are a constant planner. But even constant planners need to set aside some time to consider more carefully the notes they have made during the week.

DAILY PLANNING

Although customer records are checked at weekends, it is wiser to study each evening those applicable to the following day's work. Daily planning is, in the main, a study of customers and prospective customers. The salesperson will want to be reminded:

1. What exact services a company offers.
   If any new services have been introduced.
   If they have made known any future plans.
2. If anything has been sold to that company previously, in which case details should be available.

If there has been any complaint about the product or after-sales service.

If they can be supplied. It is not unusual for a sales agent to take an order only to find that a stop has been put on that particular account. This could be because payments are in arrears or, more usually, because it has not been possible to get extra insurance cover for them against bad debts.

If the company are prospective customers, which products will, in the main, interest the buyer.

If there are any quotations outstanding, what competitors' products they are using.

3. Who has authority to buy.
   Who could influence a buying decision.
4. Facts about a buyer – or interests.
5. Details of points discussed at a previous call.
6. Opportunities for future business.
7. The buyer's main needs.
8. The main objective of the call.
9. The secondary objective.

Demonstration Units and Sales Kits

The seller must plan the order and the way to use sales support materials. Too often a salesperson giving a demonstration says:

> 'I'm sorry it's so slow. This is new software which I only got last night.'
> 'This list of relevant references isn't perfect, but it's the best I can get.'
> 'It worked all right yesterday.'
> 'Have you a spare lead I could use?'
> 'I've only got this slightly out-of-date brochure with me.'

All equipment used for demonstration purposes must be checked over every evening, and possibly re-checked the following morning and checked again immediately after use. This is an essential part of planning.

Never risk losing a buyer's confidence by demonstrating with equipment which could be faulty. Rather, put off the demonstration. Similarly, a sales kit must be checked to be certain there are no dog-eared or stained leaflets, indecipherable drawings, or out-of-date figures.

Fashions change. Hair may be longer or shorter, trousers wider or narrower, skirts long or short, men's shirts spotted or striped, their faces shaven or bearded; but a sales kit must *always* be the same – immaculate.

PCs must be checked and batteries charged regularly. Sales literature and sales aids should always be placed in the briefcase in the same order. This enables the seller to extract the appropriate leaflet or catalogue without looking away from the buyer.

The objective of sales planning is to be prepared for every eventuality. Sales planning ensures that you give your buyer or prospective buyer the best possible service.

The salesperson who appreciates the value of pre-planning obviates guesswork, and lays the ground for success at each call.

9

The ABC of Selling

How can we find the best way to sell to every type of buyer, man or woman, store buyer or production manager, managing director or office manager, farmer or builder? Although buyers vary in shapes and sizes, moods and customs, they all buy for the same basic reason – because it benefits them or their company to do so. Each product or service has many benefits, which will be analysed later. You will be shown how to discover the main benefit of your merchandise or service. To sell perfectly on every occasion, however, you must discover the best means of explaining benefits to a buyer.

Some salespeople consider themselves well-versed in psychology, and believe they understand each customer – read his mind and tell him everything he wants to hear. This is sheer nonsense, and too many salespeople deceive themselves into believing they are mindreaders.

Back in 1934, J. B. Rhine of Duke University delved deeply into parapsychology. Many tests were carried out. The simplest involved using a pack of cards. One person chose a card and concentrated on it while a second person elsewhere attempted to read his mind and guess the card. Obviously, the tests were much more involved than this explanation suggests, but they were most stringent. It was generally agreed that there was no proof that one person could read the mind of another. [*Editor's Note:* More recent, controlled experiments could prove this to be incorrect.]

There are, of course, many recorded instances of telepathic coincidences. Someone, perhaps, has a sudden feeling that a relative is ill and later discovers that at that very moment the relative did in fact have an accident. But is this telepathy or coincidence? No one has yet given an adequate answer. If, therefore, the researchers into parapsychology cannot prove that one person can read another's mind, even when two people are in sympathy with one another, how can anyone claim that he can read the mind of a buyer?

Mindreading, however, is what some salespeople call a predictable reaction to a selling technique – but this is not mindreading; it is salesmanship. We know that a buyer is interested only in benefits. Suppose that a product has eight main benefits (which we shall call a, b, c, d, e, f, g, and h). The mindreader might estimate that the main interests of a buyer would be centred on points a, b, f, and g. He could be lucky and be right, but he could also be very wrong. Maybe the buyer's main interests were in a, b, d, and e. The mindreader would have missed out two important selling points. Wouldn't he have been wiser to explain every benefit from a to h? In that way he could dispense with mindreading or psychology; he would know that he had given the buyer every benefit and taken every opportunity to complete an order.

Friendship

Human relations coupled with a selling personality undoubtedly contribute to an order. They will not alone suffice if there is competition. Many sales agents make good friends of their customers but a buyer rarely places an order solely because of his friendly relationship with a seller. He will only do this if the 'friend' offers competitive products. The person who has won goodwill after many years of excellent service always has the advantage over a competitor.

The 'order-taker' selling consumer goods will keep his customers by friendship just so long as he has goods they want. If he changes his job and sells less competitive products, he will find that the customer, through personal regard, may give him some small orders, but the large orders will go elsewhere.

Friendship enables the seller to obtain a good hearing. After that, it is his ability that counts. Friendship alone will not necessarily sway the manager of a chain store to promote goods and indent for more, but it will get a seller a good hearing from that manager. He need only telephone a buyer for an immediate appointment, while another sales agent could be kicking his heels in a waiting-room for a long time before being seen. Many salespeople believe they are regarded highly by customers, when the reverse is true; this also applies the other way round.

Many buyers think they are liked and respected by all who call on them. Recently a buyer told me that sales agents always received fair treatment and so they would always bring him special lines. But that buyer is wrong. He is not too popular with salespeople. He breaks appointments; he is curt; he keeps them waiting unnecessarily; he is full of his own importance. Just as that buyer is mistaken, so are many salespeople who believe that a buyer is a true friend – when in reality he has a low opinion of them.

When we carried out research among buyers to test their likes and dislikes, we proved that sales staff cannot rely on friendship alone to obtain orders. We invited a panel of buyers, including managers, shop owners, garage proprietors, managing directors and store buyers, to complete a questionnaire on the buyer–seller relationship. One of the questions asked was:

What percentage of salespeople who have called on you for five years or more do you:

    like very much?
    like?
    tolerate?
    dislike?
    dislike very much?

Only six per cent came in the first group.

Experienced salespeople find it hard to accept this. They refuse to see themselves as others see them, and gradually sell less and less, until they become order-takers, remain as sales agents, and get embittered because they do not achieve promotion.

Words
There are many aids to person-to-person selling. Sales brochures, demonstration models, samples, video presentations, photographs, and drawings all play their part. Just imagine what would happen if a company produced the most elaborate and expensive sales brochure in the history of marketing. Teams of

designers laboured over it, high-profile photographers were commissioned, and the brochure was printed in the Far East using the latest technology.

At last it is out, and a copy is sent to a salesperson. He approaches a customer and, lips tightly shut, produces the brochure. He indicates various illustrations and captions, saying nothing. He relies entirely on the brochure to sell his goods for him.

Will he take an order? Certainly not! The customer would not read all the printed matter and, although perhaps interested in the beautiful layout and photography, and full of admiration for the design, he would not make a decision on such incomplete evidence. He would need explanations – he would raise objections and would want answers. If this were not so, every company would merely produce such a brochure and post it to a buyer, and expect an order by return of post.

While such a sales aid might help a salesperson, it can do no more. If the seller does not speak, he cannot sell.

A salesperson is paid to sell – and that means, to talk. He may make a living without using a single sales aid, but a sales aid alone cannot earn a living for a seller who doesn't make use of the right words at the right time. *A salesperson, therefore, lives by the words he uses.*

You must agree with that. You will also agree that if you knew that certain words had sales appeal while others did not register, you would use only words that brought positive results. You might find these words were not helping your sale along:

I wonder . . .
I think . . .
I hope . . .
Possibly, it . . .

In their place, you could say:

I am sure that . . .
I know . . .
I am certain . . .
It will . . .

You will use these words because you have confidence in your goods. If you haven't, you shouldn't be selling them. A seller succeeds because he chooses the right words and bans all negative words. But he doesn't use words in isolation. They are strung together to become compelling sentences. Almost every word a sales agent uses should help him towards his objective. Every sentence should condition the mind of the buyer towards acceptance of his offer.

A seller must have the stamina to be able to fight back when that big order is lost – he must strive for his objectives in spite of continual government-inspired constraints. He should be sincere, and look presentable – but if he cannot select the right words to answer an objection or to stress the benefits of his products, he cannot succeed.

Consider the words given below (they are not 'opposites') and then decide that you will only use words and phrases which have the qualities listed in the left-hand column:

appropriate words	*ambiguous words*
certain	casual
common-sense	careless
comprehensive	boastful
constructive	bitter
descriptive	doubtful
keen	boring
explicit	faltering
vibrant	frivolous
good	futile
honest	flattering
impressive	blundering
clear	incoherent
significant	obsolete
powerful	pathetic
stirring	pompous
direct	superfluous
strong	trite
understandable	incomprehensible

appropriate words	*ambiguous words*
vivid	vague
attractive	weird
appropriate	angry
creative	wondering
impressive	half-hearted
emphatic	pessimistic

A Logical Pattern

'I never forget a face,' says one person, and adds, 'but I just can't remember names.' Another will tell you that she always forgets birthdays, and a third will say ruefully that he sometimes can't even remember his own telephone number.

All of us, on occasion, have been asked by a stranger for directions to a street we pass every day, but when the request is made we feel like foreigners in our own locality – we just can't remember where the street is located.

There are many reasons given for a lapse of memory, but we are not concerned with the jargon of psychologists explaining temporary amnesia, or with the platitudes of the teacher: 'You are not paying attention – that is why you cannot remember.' We have to concentrate only on the solution, and a solution must be found to enable the seller to remember every facet of his product or service, and all the benefits derived from them.

Many a seller has said to himself after leaving a buyer without an order, 'I forgot to tell him . . .' or, 'Why didn't I tell him . . .?' or 'If only I had explained . . .'

While selling, we cannot consult a checklist of benefits. The most we can do is to glance occasionally at a leaflet, but that could never do more than partly solve the problem of remembering the complete sales offer – and, to succeed, a seller must remember all the benefits, at every call. Equally important, he must present them in a logical sequence.

There are occasions when the sequence should be changed. For example, when a product has several different applications, the main benefit for one buyer could be a subsidiary benefit for another. As a seller should always begin his offer with a main benefit rather than stressing a minor point, this might need a reversal of the usual order.

If a minor benefit is given in the first place the interest of the buyer can be lost; but by commencing with the main benefit the seller holds the attention of the buyer, who should want to hear more.

For example, a sales agent may be selling an industrial catering service. Perhaps his main feature is that his company will supply fully trained cafeteria staff. However, he may know in advance that a prospect is dissatisfied with the lack of menu variety supplied by a competitor. If the seller is confident that his company can give the variety required, it would be right for him to make this his main and first feature when he calls. But it is usually unnecessary to alter the order of benefits in a sales offer. If a salesperson switches the benefit order at almost every call he will, inevitably, forget some aspect of his product which might motivate a buyer to buy.

It is important, therefore, that a seller should arrange his benefits in a logical pattern. All of us form a logical sequence in our mind whenever we want to make a request.

For example, if we require a bank loan, we do not, without thought, hurry to the bank, ask to see the manager, and immediately ask him for a loan. Long before we are due to meet, we will have turned over and over in our mind exactly what we are going to say. We plant in our memory cells all the main reasons why we need a new car, an extension to the house, or extra stock for our business. Then we bring a pattern to these mental pictures, so that we have a story with a beginning, a middle, and an end – in logical sequence. We even decide on the type of friendly greeting we shall use.

We build confidence by telling him how well we are doing. We extol the great advantages to us of having a new car – how it will increase our business, protect our health . . . Or we explain the extra value of our property from an extension we intend building. We conclude by telling him the ease with which we can make repayments. Because we have rehearsed it in our mind so often, we remember it word for word, and the bank manager, whether he grants the loan or not, will hear the full story.

We do not say subsequently, 'I wish I'd told him . . .'

It is one of the important aids to a seller's memory to be able to repeat his sales offer again and again in a similar pattern. There can be many interruptions and many variations during a sale, but if a product has twenty benefits, the salesperson must present those twenty benefits to the buyer, giving them in a logical order so that he is unlikely to forget any part of his sales offer.

It is so natural for us to think in a logical order – that is the way our memory cells work. Here is an exercise to prove this point.

Answer quickly:

> *Give as rapidly as possible all the numbers between one and ten.*

Automatically, you repeated *one, two, three, four, five, six* . . . You didn't mouth *eight, seven, five, six*, or begin at *ten* and work backwards. You thought of consecutive numbers because it was rational to do so.

In the same way, you will be able to remember all your benefits when you organise them from *one to ten, one to twenty*, or *one to thirty* – however many you may have.

Key Sentences

A key sentence is a simple sentence related to a fact or feature of the product, which reminds the seller of that fact or feature, and the benefits related to it. As many sentences should be evolved as there are benefits.

Call back to your mind the first few words of the proverb, *Early to bed, early to rise* . . . Automatically into your mind flashes *makes a man healthy, wealthy, and wise.*

Once a key sentence is remembered it is almost impossible to stop the flow of words which build and elaborate on that sentence.

Here is another example: *A bird in the hand* . . . Could you stop yourself continuing with *is worth two in the bush?* You almost certainly murmured those words to yourself automatically.

Ask anyone over 60 to tell you the name of a well-known song from a very old musical show, *The Bing Boys*, that was staged about 1915. Few will be able to remember a song written so many years before they were born; but ask those same people to give you the next line from a song beginning *If you were the only girl in the world* . . . and seven out of ten will continue *and I was the only boy*. These are the opening words of the song from that very, very old musical, *The Bing Boys*.

This is proof of how key sentences act as a reminder, and unlock the memory. It is a technique developed by TACK over the years, and is now used by salespeople all over the world as a memory aid.

Here are some key sentences:

A salesperson is selling a new external wall paint. The paint has a very important feature, eliminating the need for a lot of preparation work, including priming and sealing. An easily remembered key sentence could be:

> *You don't have to prime or seal.*

This immediately highlights the obvious benefits of:

> *saving time* – important in factory maintenance
> *saving labour* – a very big benefit indeed, where maintenance labour is scarce
> *saving materials* – primer and paint in one tin
> *a considerable saving on the hire of scaffolding.*

With that single easily remembered sentence, a seller can pinpoint the YOU appeal so vital in his presentation.

A salesperson offering catering services to industry could use this sentence:

> *Quality meals for your staff under your own roof.*

These few words remind the seller of the many factors which would show benefits to the buyer:

> The *quality* of the meals, which would ensure no complaints
> The *consistency* of the service
> The *efficiency* that backs it

The dangers of staff having to go out at midday, skipping meals, and therefore producing less work during the afternoon (own roof)

Staff who go out and arrive back late because of difficulty of getting a meal locally (own roof)

The effect on staff of seeing that management have their interests at heart (quality)

The retention of key personnel through this additional welfare (your staff)

Easier recruitment by offering extra facilities.

An excellent key sentence used by a company called Dunlop was:

Dunlop Thixofix spreads like butter – grips like iron.

After voicing that sentence, no seller could fail to describe vividly the ease of application and the many uses of Thixofix.

The ABC of Selling

Remembering the benefit sequence, the salesperson will be able to present his case to the buyer in a logical, clear, and progressive manner, while averting the constrictions of a rigid sales formula.

Steps to the Order

Over the years, many a sales formula has been developed to enable a salesperson to be logical in his presentation. The basic idea behind every standard sequence is that it should concentrate the seller's mind on the selling fundamentals so that he can present his case in a logical and orderly manner. But helpful as they were, they were not the complete answer to the salesperson's problem, which is reminding himself of the steps he must cover if he is to give a complete sales offer.

Let us consider some of the *steps to the order* which have been used over the past twenty years:

attention
interest
desire
action.

How can *attention* be separated from *interest*? It is only possible to hold a buyer's attention by creating immediate interest. So these two steps must be combined.

Logically there can be no reason for a separate step *desire*. *Desire* (*want* is a more appropriate word) must be created from the opening of the sale to the close. There cannot be only one step devoted to persuading the buyer to *want* a product or service.

Here is another example:

> approach
> creating interest
> creating confidence
> selling the product benefits
> creating desire ·
> close.

In this sequence, there is an additional step – *creation of confidence*.

This is undoubtedly a move in the right direction, because it reminds a seller of the need, whether he is well known or unknown to a buyer) whether he has been calling on a company for year or weeks, to maintain confidence always.

It is right, therefore, for all salespeople to *create confidence* quickly, but if the seller leaves it at that he may, possibly, not take away the buyer's concern (new accounts had been known to let him down in the past). So again, creating confidence cannot be a single step, it must be established and re-established throughout the sale.

Here is another example:

> introduction
> finding needs
> benefits
> investment
> close.

It is surely wrong to label the opening remarks of a seller as *introduction*. It is true he is introducing his sales offer to the buyer, but no one is introducing him to the buyer. The word *introduction* itself seems to be a relic of the nineteenth century, when sales staff wore top hats.

Finding needs is an essential step in selling, but whenever possible a seller should discover the *needs* before the call is made. This is a part of sales planning. If a buyer's needs are unknown a seller cannot ask the direct question, 'What are your needs?' The true need may take a long time to establish.

Investment, on the face of it, is a good step. It is right to prove to a buyer that he is not only buying to fill an immediate need, but he is making a safe investment for the future. But this is a benefit that might have to be established quite early in the sales offer. There is no reason why suddenly, towards the end of the sale, the seller should explain the benefit of investment.

Here is another example:

    attention
    interest
    conviction
    action

Every seller should offer proof to substantiate the claims he is making. Sales points can be proved by the use of testimonial letters – letters of reference – copies of a paper written by an authority on the subject – articles in trade journals – research reports – Government reports . . . but the offering of such proof is not a separate step. Every benefit given must carry *conviction*, and the proof should be given to a buyer point by point.

After many years of teaching and research we know that separate steps no longer apply – steps to remind the seller to *create confidence*, to *emphasise benefits*, to *summarise*, to *create interest* – any more than there is a need for a separate step for a seller to *answer objections*.

For all that, every attempt to find the ideal sequence has been helpful to salespeople. From the days of scripts to be learned and spoken parrotwise by sales agents, many ideas have been evolved and tried with varying success. Most of them failed to be the complete answer because they were too rigid, too impersonal, too unnatural, and difficult to remember. Nevertheless, a seller must have guide lines if his presentation is not to lack impact.

TACK Training have always believed that selling should be made easy rather than difficult, and we are always researching to this end. The ideal is for a salesperson to use his personality to good effect, which is not possible if strictures are placed on him. For a seller to be told exactly what he has to say is straight-jacketing his mind.

TACK believe that although a sales manager may provide his sales staff with guidelines, he should not attempt to put a set of words into their mouths. A seller must evolve *his* own sentences, his *own* manner of elaborating benefits derived from features.

We know that a salesperson should sell conversationally. We know that by repetition he will present his benefits in a logical order. We know that by memorising key sentences he will be able to elaborate each benefit, giving the maximum YOU appeal.

The object of the *opening* is to hold the undivided *attention* of the buyer. The object of the *close* is to obtain a *decision*.

Sandwiched in between are all the *benefits*. And to ensure that not a single feature is omitted nor a benefit forgotten, all benefits should be presented in a logical sequence.

It's literally 'as simple as ABC' –

Attention
Benefits
Close.

These are the only steps a seller has to remember to enable him to succeed in selling.

10

The Opening . . . Getting the Buyer's Attention

When you do not have someone's attention, you are selling under adverse conditions. If the conditions are wrong, you can rarely persuade anyone to do anything.

Self-made Adverse Conditions
A seller can create adverse conditions for himself during the first few seconds of an interview:

1. By *looking hopelessly around the buyer's office for somewhere to park his soaking wet coat or umbrella*. A seller should always leave his coat/umbrella outside the buyer's office, whenever possible.
2. By *slamming the door behind him*. A slammed door can cause intense annoyance to a buyer.
3. By *gabbling*. When a seller speaks too quickly or slurs his opening words, a buyer will not strain to hear what is being said. His attention will wander, and he may cut the interview short.

   Many salespeople let their words pour out when they meet a buyer for the first time, or when hoping to close a big order. This is due to nervousness, from which even the most experienced of sales agents is not immune. The seller should not enunciate every word as if the buyer were a moron, but neither should he gabble. He need only speak a little more slowly than usual.

4. By *using weak or insulting sentences*. 'Insults?', you may exclaim, 'Nonsense! No seller begins by insulting a buyer.' To this reasonable assumption he should add the word *knowingly*.

Here are some examples of insulting openings:

> 'I was just passing by and thought you would want to see me about . . .'
> 'I thought I'd just pop in to ask if . . .'

To the mind of a buyer these remarks imply that his business, in the view of the seller, does not warrant a special call. Also, this type of sentence undermines the self-importance of the buyer.

Neither should a salesperson use a semi-apologetic opening:

> 'If I'm not troubling you too much . . .'
> 'I wonder if you would mind . . .'
> 'Forgive me if I'm intruding on your time, but . . .'

Weak openings only diminish the seller in the mind of the buyer.

Never make adverse conditions for yourself.

BUYER-GENERATED ADVERSE CONDITIONS

A *buyer-generated adverse condition* is any situation in which a seller, *through no fault of his own*, finds it impossible to obtain the undivided attention of the buyer.

For example, you might greet an IT Manager when his network has just 'crashed', a Human Resources Director when there has just been a serious staff injury, or a Chief Accountant when a major customer has just gone into liquidation while owing a lot of money. Your approach will fall on deaf ears. The prospect is then much more interested in her situation than in you. You may well find yourself standing on the pavement with a hearing refused, with the buyer closing the door behind her. In this case, you must first get back into the office before beginning to sell again.

When the buyer is preoccupied, don't begin to sell until she has finished whatever she is doing. When the production manager is helping one of his staff with a problem, stand aside until he has given his advice, and then try to lead him back to his office.

Here are other examples – problems and solutions which have been provided by delegates at our Selling to Industry and Commerce course:

Selling on the Shop Floor
The reason for your visit is to finalise an order. You have an appointment to see Production Director John Brown. You arrive five minutes before the appointed time to be told by the receptionist that Mr Brown is in A shop. As you are well known to her,she suggests that it would save time, as you have the appointment, if you went upstairs and waited for Mr Brown outside his office.

There, you meet his PA, Ms Howell, who tells you that Mr Brown will be at least another 30 minutes, and adds, 'Would you rather make another appointment? Or, if you care to, you can go down to A shop . . .'

You decide to visit the factory floor. On arrival at A shop you see Mr Brown in conversation with three supervisors. Approaching them and realising that they are having a heated discussion, you back away and ask a fitter standing nearby if there is a crisis.

He tells you that there is trouble because a vital new computer has broken down.

Mr Brown sees you and calls out, 'I won't be a few minutes and I'll be with you . . .'

What do you do?

1. Wait for Mr Brown to be free?
2. Return to his office and wait for him there?
3. Make an appointment for another occasion?

The decision of the delegate was to return to Mr Brown's office and leave a short note for him. He wrote:

> *I appreciate your willingness to keep the appointment, but realise you have to give priority to the problems on the shop floor. I thought, therefore, you would prefer me to call again and see you later in the week.*

Ms Howell has suggested that Friday at 11 a.m. may be convenient for you, and I shall telephone her this afternoon to confirm if this is so.

The delegate believed that if he had attempted to finalise details of the new installation on the shop floor he would have failed. He also believed that even if Mr Brown had accompanied him to his office, the buyer would still have been thinking about whether or not he had settled the problem in A Shop.

The delegate said he will never know whether or not he would have got the order if he had stayed, but that he *did* get it when he called on the following Friday.

Selling in the Factory Cafeteria

The competition has been intense, but you are confident that you have won a very large order for paper shredders. When you call on Bill Roberts, the managing director, for final approval, he keeps you waiting for some time, then apologises and invites you to have lunch with him. 'Over lunch,' he said, 'you can answer the few remaining questions still in my mind.'

Roberts, in his early thirties, is a self-made entrepreneur, strong-minded, determined, but a very friendly person. You have met him twice previously, and although he made it clear on each occasion that he was not prepared to have his time wasted and that he wanted direct answers to direct questions, you felt sure you had impressed him.

Instead of taking you to a private restaurant, he conducts you to the staff cafeteria on the top floor. In one corner of the cafeteria-cum-restaurant, the tables are occupied by the company's executives. Reading your mind, he says, 'We're all workers here – I don't believe in executives eating in lavishly decorated rooms. Actually, it's very good of our staff to allow us to eat with them.'

You laugh dutifully. He guides you to a table with seating for eight. Six of the seats are already occupied. After shaking hands with the six others, three of whom you have already met, you are led to the self-service counter to collect your meal.

Soon after returning to the table, the bantering begins. They rib each other, and then gently pull your leg about the ethics of salespeople.

After a while, Roberts says, 'I want you to tell me again why you think your shredders are better than those made by X, which cost 15 per cent less.'

One of the executives says, 'They both shred papers. Five per cent I could understand, but how can you possibly justify 15 per cent more?'

Do you immediately answer the question raised by the executive?

Do you again sell Roberts and all his colleagues on the benefits of your shredders?

Do you talk to the table in general?

Do you concentrate on the executive who emphasised the difference in cost of the two machines?

Or, do you make an attempt to get away from the group?

The course delegate told us that he knew that if he became involved in a cut-and-thrust discussion with the executives they would do their best to pull his story to pieces, if only to prove to Bill Roberts what keen minds they had.

He said to the managing director, 'Mr Roberts, it would not be helpful to you or your colleagues if I were to detail the value and benefits of our shredders to you now. I left my case in your office and in that case is back-up evidence to justify your buying our *quality* shredder. Without that evidence you could come to the wrong decision, and that would be unfair to you. When I called previously, Mr Roberts, you insisted that you only wanted to hear facts. I promise you that when we return to your office I can give you all the facts you require, to prove that we can offer you the best value on the market.'

To the delegate's delight Mr Roberts said, 'I agree,' and then switched the conversation, and other matters were discussed. On returning to the managing director's office, the order was signed.

Never in the Corridor

You call to see a financial director, Doreen Hardy, to progress the sale of some new software in which she is interested. She is a difficult person to sell to because on each occasion you have seen her she has thought of new applications for the software.

On your way to his office you meet her in a corridor and she says, 'You're the very man I want to see. I'm concerned about the input . . .'

Do you listen to her query and deal with it on the spot?

Do you suggest that it is very difficult to show her the necessary specification while standing in the corridor, and it would be better if you both went to her office?

The delegate told us that he took the first course and dealt with the problem. Ms Hardy then raised another point. The discussion lasted some fifteen minutes, after which she made an excuse, shook hands with the delegate, and walked quickly away.

Eventually, the order went to a competitor.

He believed that one of the reasons he lost the sale was because he was at a distinct disadvantage while selling in the corridor. The interview had been cut short just when he was about to press home some of the strongest benefits of his solution. If they had been in Ms Hardy's office the delegate would not have been summarily dismissed and could have found out her real objection to placing the order.

Buyers often make a point of seeing a seller in a waiting-room, entrance hall, or corridor, because they know that they can always walk away. This is the most common of all *buyer-generated adverse conditions*.

There are many other examples of adverse conditions: when a buyer is about to leave for home – when the cafeteria manager is extremely busy, between twelve noon and two p.m. – when the warehouse manager is involved with an awkward delivery problem . . .

If you consider the conditions for selling are adverse it is better not to begin to sell,

BUT

it isn't always easy to decide whether or not the conditions are adverse. A seller must not always believe a buyer who says, 'I'm very busy,' or 'I can only spare five minutes,' or 'I have another appointment shortly.' The buyer may just be seeking an excuse to get rid of a seller *before* he has heard his proposition. Buyers delight in creating adverse conditions, but they can be overcome by a salesperson's ability to sell well and to create immediate interest in his offer.

When in doubt, stay put. When you know that the odds are really against your being able to explain your proposition, or that it is impossible to hold the buyer's attention because of his *real* preoccupation with other matters, then leave him, and try again another day.

THE FIRST CALL

All salespeople have to make first-time calls at some time or another, but whether a seller meets a buyer for the first time or the hundredth time, he still has to gain, and hold, the buyer's attention during the first minutes of the meeting. On the majority of occasions a busy buyer wants a seller to explain quickly the purpose of his visit, but there is a friendly type of buyer who doesn't mind a few pleasantries before learning of the salesperson's offer. These pleasantries, whether lasting seconds or minute's can be called the *chat gap*.

Sometimes a courteous and friendly type of buyer, when first meeting a seller, will offer him a seat and make some relaxing comment, such as: 'What a day! Did you get very wet walking from our car park? It's too far away from the factory block . . .'

This is an invitation for the seller to reassure the buyer, in the fewest possible words, that all is well and he did not get really wet because he had an umbrella/mac, which he left in the waiting-room/hall/corridor . . . But the buyer's friendly greeting is not an invitation for the seller to relate what happened once when he called at a factory whose car park was even further away from the factor block . . .

At a first call, except when a buyer indulges in a few pleasant words, the salesperson should determine to gain the buyer's undivided attention with his opening sentence. The *chat gap*, however, may lengthen when the seller calls back regularly on the buyer.

Over the years a friendship may develop which would make it ridiculous for the seller to attempt to grip the buyer's immediate attention. The buyer may have been ill, away on holiday, or at a conference. He may have been honoured in some way, or his wife may have had a baby. It is, then, only natural for the salesperson to begin by saying, 'Are you quite well again now?' or, 'Was it a boy?' or, 'You were very good on TV last Wednesday.'

There is nothing wrong with such friendly remarks, but again, the objective of the seller is to keep them short. By keeping to one simple rule a sales agent can always be sure of reducing the length of the *chat gap*. The rule is:

> *Never, never talk about yourself – your interests – your hobbies – your holidays – your family – your car – your accident – your health . . . Never give your opinion uninvited on the political situation – the election – or world affairs . . .*

If you do, the *chat gap* will lengthen and you will, inevitably, bore the buyer. Even if the buyer asks you about yourself out of politeness – your hobbies, children, etc. – answer in as few words as possible. 'They're fine, thank you,' is quite enough. He doesn't really want to hear more, he is only being polite.

If a seller is foolish enough to talk about himself he can be certain of one fact: the buyer won't listen and will, possibly, cut short the interview saying, 'I'm so sorry but I have to leave you, I have another appointment . . .'

Because it is so difficult for anybody to believe that lessons in human relations apply to them, many sales agents will say, 'But in my case it is different – my buyers like to hear about my . . .'

They do not.

GETTING ATTENTION

Whether the *chat gap* lasts five seconds or five minutes, as soon as it ends it is vital for the seller to gain the buyer's attention by interesting him in the opening of his sales offer. There are five proven techniques, each of which can enable a seller to hold the buyer's attention time and time again. These techniques can be used at the first call or at the tenth call.

Here they are:

> the factual opening
> the question opening
> the reference opening
> the sales aid opening
> the demonstration opening.

And for those who call back regularly on their clients, there is an additional technique which can be used:

> the link opening.

Factual Opening

All of us have an insatiable desire to learn facts about subjects which interest us. What other reason is there for *The Guinness Book of Records* being a world bestseller? If we are sending our child to a new school, all the facts we can gather about that school are read avidly. If someone is considering emigrating he will read every fact he can about the country in which he hopes, eventually, to live. Just think of the brochures we study when we are planning a holiday abroad. We lap up the facts . . . six miles of sand, a hundred and fifty-two restaurants, eight golf courses, four swimming pools . . .

Why should a buyer be any different in his thinking? We know he is no different, that he is motivated in the same way as all of us. A buyer's attention can always be held by a fact, or a series of facts, if they are directly connected with his business; and his attention is just as likely to be held by a fact which concerns his business on the fiftieth call as one which interested him on the first call.

Here are some examples of factual openings:

'Ms Brown, it is a fact that oil fuels contain more energy in a given volume than any other fuel, but not all fuels are consistent and dependable. With X, we guarantee . . .'

'A recent survey showed that 28 per cent of companies never obtain competitive guides for their fleet insurance. We get those competitive quotes on your behalf.'

'There is now a way of fixing very heavy objects to a cavity wall without having to use special plugs or studding . . .'

'Mr Smith, in a recent report from the World Health Council it was stated that noise was a main cause of stress in business. Our triple glazing will . . .'

'Mrs Williams, you can now have up to 1,500 internal telephone extensions. As your plant covers so many acres I am sure you will be interested in our new . . .'

'It is an unfortunate fact, Mr Johnson, as you know, that vandals are continually breaking factory windows on this estate. It need not happen to your factory any more, because we have a new glass . . .'

'It is not generally known, Mr Jennings, but one electric convection oven can cook eight hundred meals in eight minutes . . .'

'Good morning, Mr Jeweller. With every expanding watch-bracelet you sell there is a hidden extra five per cent profit for you.'

'Good morning, Ms Jones. I have been outside your shop for five minutes. During that time seventy-four people passed by – that is eight hundred and eighty-eight an hour. Do you know that many more of them could be induced to stop and look in your window?'

'Good morning, Mr Hosier. It is a major expense, as you know, to send back faulty shirts to the manufacturers. At our factory, returns are negligible because of the great care we take in manufacture and testing.'

'Good morning, Ms Office Manager. You can now have just one unit, not only for all faxes and copying, but also to handle multiple runs and special colour designs which used to require very expensive printing machines. I am from . . .'

'One of the difficulties of handling frozen foodstuffs is that the limited amount of storage space often restricts the variety you can handle. We have just instituted a daily delivery scheme using insulated vans with every variety of frozen product . . .'

'Scaffolding equipment is usually required at short notice in the building trade, but only the larger builders can afford to buy adequate stocks. My company, XYZ Scaffolding Ltd, operate an extremely attractive rental scheme with depots strategically placed throughout the country to supply your needs within hours . . .'

The Question Opening

Ask a silly question and you'll get a silly answer is an old tag, but conversely, and equally true is: ask a sensible or serious question, and you will always get a sensible answer.

Only those facing interrogation refuse to answer questions. The rest of us do so with pleasure, either instantly, or after some thought.

When we are in a furniture shop and the assistant says, 'What is the present colour scheme in your bedroom?' we are eager to tell her the design of our curtains, the colouring of the carpet, the matching tones of the upholstery and the wallpaper . . .

One simple question involves us immediately in her sales offer.

If the car salesperson asks us, 'Will you be using the car abroad as well as in this country?' we can hardly wait to tell him of our projected tour across Europe.

Buyers always react to a question by becoming involved in the sale. Whether you have to influence the mind of a purchasing manager, personnel officer, design engineer, project engineer – if you ask him a question you will immediately obtain his undivided attention. Don't be concerned, however, at the brevity of his reply. He is involved in the sale. He might answer at length, but even if he only says, 'Yes' or 'No', it still allows you to elaborate, and you will have achieved your objective.

Here are some examples:

'Mr Smith, is it right that from this factory you export to nearly every part of the world?'

'Yes, we're very proud of our exporting achievements.'

'Then you will be interested to hear of our new daily world-wide cargo flights . . .'

* * *

'Mrs Kendal, am I right in saying that it is essential for you to use refrigerated vans for delivery?'

'Yes.'

'Then you will be interested in our . . .'

* * *

'Mr Laurie, I am sure you will agree that everyone, these days, should consider ways of reducing pollution.'

'Yes, I certainly agree with that.'

'Well, we have designed a revolutionary exhaust system to eliminate completely those intensely choking diesel fumes. Our new . . .'

* * *

'Mr Brown, is it right that one of your main problems is the risk of water getting into the bearings?'

'That's a problem we always have.'

'Well, Mr Brown, our new plastic-covered bearings can relieve you of that worry, because . . .'

* * *

'Miss King, can your present photocopier copy right up to the spine of a ledger?'

'No.'

'But you do think it would be helpful to you if it did?'

'Yes, on occasion perhaps.'

'Well, our new Fotoit will . . .'

*   *   *

'Mrs Staples, do you agree that dynamic, expanding businesses like yours need up-to-the-minute financial information at very short notice?'

'Of course, it is essential.'

'Well, Mrs Staples, providing up-to-the-minute information on foreign exchange rules systems is our business . . .'

*   *   *

'Mr Electrical Dealer, would you agree that your shelf space is highly valuable to you?'

The retailer must answer, 'Yes.'

'If then,' the salesperson continues, 'you could display the same products and still have 20 per cent space available for other goods, you would think it worth while, wouldn't you?'

'Yes.'

'Our new lamps are 20 per cent smaller than those we used to make, but they have the same output and last just as long. You will not only find them quick-moving, but as they take up so much less space on your shelves you will have more room to display more goods. I am from . . .'

*   *   *

'Can you sell many high-quality power drills to your current customers?'

This question prompts two thoughts in the prospect's mind. First, 'This person doesn't think I can sell high-quality products – I'll show him I can.' Second, 'He must be very certain of the quality of his products to ask me such a question.'

When he answers 'Yes', the seller continues, 'Then, sir, I

can show you how you can make extra profit by selling the most expensive but the finest quality drill on the market. I am from . . .'

*   *   *

'Good morning, Dr Brown. Isn't it true, doctor, that more and more patients visit your surgery suffering from migraine?'

'Yes, it is a growing modern complaint.'

'Well, Dr Brown, as you may know, we have developed a new treatment about which an article appeared in the *Lancet* recently, and I should like to amplify one or two of the points made in it . . .'

*   *   *

'Mr Giles, would you agree that the biggest overhead in farming today is labour costs?'

'Yes, I suppose so.'

'Well, we now act as distributors for Better Fertilisers Ltd, which has produced a new fertiliser which is so concentrated that much less labour is needed to spread it, but it is more effective than the normal type of fertiliser . . .'

*   *   *

'Do you agree that your job as a retailer is made much easier by manufacturers who go all out to stimulate public demand for their products?'

'Yes, that is so.'

'Well, my company now conducts the biggest advertising campaign in the trade, and I would like to give you details of our new programme for the next three months.'

*   *   *

'Ms Smith, isn't it your experience that a very large proportion of men's toiletries are purchased by women?'

'Yes, that is true.'

'It is because of this that XYZ have designed their products for men, but with women in mind. Let me show you an example of the new type of pack we have produced . . .'

*   *   *

There is, of course, a similarity between stating a fact and asking a question. A fact can be turned into a question, in the same way as many questions can be changed into facts. But there is one difference in these openings: with the Question Opening the salesperson expects, and gets, a reply. With the Factual Opening he states the fact, arouses the buyer's interest, but does not pause for an answer. He continues with his sales offer.

The Reference Opening
What is the ideal attention-getting technique? If used properly, it is the Reference Opening.

Let us think again of what immediately interests us. When considering a holiday in some sun-baked Mediterranean resort, we cannot make up our minds which of the hotels in the package deal to choose; and then a friend says to us, 'You must stay at the Capitol Hotel, it's absolutely marvellous. The food is wonderful and the service can't be bettered. Do you know they even . . .'

Do we hesitate? Not for a moment! We book up at the Capitol and tell everyone we meet that we are staying at a highly recommended hotel.

If we need dental treatment and a friend says, 'You should go to Mrs Williams in the High Street – she is the most marvellous dentist I've ever known. She hates giving you pain. You know how nervous I am generally . . .'

Off we go to meet Mrs Williams.

And what do we do when a business acquaintance says, 'Why don't you go and see Mr Lane of Kerr Brothers about this? It seems just right for him. He's a friend of mine – mention my name.'

We very quickly telephone Mr Lane for an appointment, and Mr Lane will, undoubtedly, see us, because he knows his friend wouldn't waste his time.

The mind of the buyer is always influenced by a recommendation from someone he knows. It can also be influenced if he is shown, very early in the interview, a letter stressing the benefits of your products, written by an executive of a company of repute.

But never use a letter written by a buyer's competitor. That could antagonise him.

Also, be careful about showing a letter from a giant organisation to the managing director employing some fifty people. His response could be, 'It's all right for them with their millions, but we are not big enough.'

The Sales Aid Opening

Scene I. Father is in the kitchen studying the football results. Mother enters, accompanied by daughter. The daughter places on the table a large irregular-shaped parcel. Father glances at it, then returns to the pools. He glances again at the parcel. Eventually, even the report on a key match involving his home team cannot hold him. 'What's in that?' he asks his daughter, pointing at the parcel.

* * *

Scene II. The managing director is reading through important documents. Her assistant enters and places on her desk a large 'Private and Confidential' envelope.

Turning away from the important documents, she asks, 'What's in that?'

What is it that makes husbands put down newspapers and tycoons turn away from important matters?

Curiosity!

When a buyer sees a sales agent unwrapping a small parcel, or opening a case in which something gleams brightly, or taking a plastic container from his pocket, that buyer will not want the seller to leave before he has found out what it is that is gleaming in the leather case – what new concept is in the plastic container – what is so special about that parcel . . .

The Sales Aid Opening, being based on the natural curiosity of most people, will always get a buyer's undivided attention.

When the buyer sees an agent taking from his case a well-designed leaflet or an appealing brochure, curiosity and interest are aroused. When he is handed a piece of material he is curious to discover its benefits for himself. If he is purchasing industrial perfume for use in a new product, his sense of smell will quickly involve him in the sales offer. An agent selling foodstuffs to an industrial cafeteria manager will find that tasting allows the buyer to sell himself on the flavour; and a buyer will strain to hear if a seller shows apparatus claimed to be almost silent in operation.

If by using a sales aid you can cover all the prospect's five senses – sight, touch, taste, smell, and hearing – you will make a very good opening. This can rarely be achieved, but the objective should be to appeal to as many of the senses as possible.

Catalogues, descriptions or specifications of equipment, photographs of installations, independent test reports, performance graphs, reproductions of testimonial letters from well-known companies can be used as a Sales Aid Opener.

Agents selling to retailers and wholesalers will have samples of their range – especially new products – which would obviously be shown.

Also used currently by sales staff at the opening are:

- A sample six-inch square showing the formation of the joint of the tongue-and-groove flooring laminate
- Example of use of paper, e.g., airline brochure
- Photograph of a hotel
- Small length of hose and coupling to show construction and quality
- Sample of special weld blending
- Fabrics
- All types of electronic components
- Mouldings.

You do not want the buyer, at the opening, to read through a brochure line by line – he would only pretend to do so, anyway. When using literature as a Sales Aid Opening, the seller must pinpoint one particular feature applicable to the buyer's business. The seller should always maintain control of the interview by holding the leaflet and pointing out the features. He should not hand it over for the buyer to study, enabling him to glance casually at each page, which half-hearted interest could lead him to decide that he is not interested.

The Sales Aid Opening can be most effective if linked with a Factual, or Question Opening.

The Demonstration Opening

Pen and paper can provide an excellent Demonstration Opening, which can immediately involve a buyer in the sales offer.

A salesperson's opening sentence could be:

> 'We can move ten of your crates in ten minutes. Overall, this will mean a saving in time of . . .'

The salesperson then writes down the total number of crates handled in a week and begins working out the overall saving in time. And from then on to cost reduction (continually involving the buyer in the calculations).

If, however, you are able to demonstrate equipment, the buyer will be quickly involved so there is very little need for attention-getting sentences.

Here are examples used by sales agents:

- Cut-away model of electronic solenoid control valves
- Booster amplifiers to simulate operation
- Scale-model motorised sweeper
- Working model of ultrasonic level control
- Internal bathroom air extractor unit with timing device
- 'Lego' for demonstrating a layout of warehouses, showing racking systems, etc.
- Small-scale working model of generator plant to show

different areas that could need monitoring

When demonstrating at the opening of a sale, remember these points:

1. Never demonstrate with an imperfect unit.
2. Whenever possible, let the buyer sell himself on the unit by allowing him to work the model.
3. Demonstrate very slowly. Make sure that your prospect is following each point, by asking him questions.

Sometimes it is better to list features/benefits of a unit before the demonstration takes place. On other occasions, however, a Demonstration Opening can be most effective, with each benefit being stressed as the demonstration progresses.

CALLING BACK

There are many reasons for industrial sales agents calling back on prospective buyers or customers, but whatever the objective, they can all be termed *Development Calls*. At every contact, high or low, a seller attempts to develop the worth and profitability of the relationship.

Here are some examples:

To negotiate long-term business
To get products or services specified
To get repeat orders
To close orders after days, weeks, months, of negotiation
To carry out a survey
To see those who can influence decisions
To try once more to open an account
To introduce new units in a range
To handle a complaint
To discover the real reason why a competitor is obtaining business (buyers rarely give the real reason for changing)
To obtain goodwill by showing operators how to get the best out of equipment sold

> *To get an introduction to another buyer*
> *To make certain that customers know all the benefits of products and the*
> *full range of company's services, when taking over a new territory*
> *To gain knowledge of production conditions*
> *To get agreement to visit a factory or stage a demonstration of equipment*
> *To establish with design department further needs*
> *To introduce new lines*
> *To get agreement from production manager to allow a visit to works by*
> *prospective buyer*
> *To present quotation, specification, costings changes in schedule*

Let us consider three of these objectives, and how they can be tackled by salespeople:

1. *To maintain goodwill and keep out competition by showing machine operators (or any other employees) how to get the best out of the equipment.*

Does the salesperson approach the machinists (having first, of course, obtained permission) and say, 'I know you're all a bit thick, so I thought I'd call to show you how to obtain the best results from the equipment . . .' or, 'It hardly seems possible, but even now some of you don't know the full capabilities of the equipment!'

You can imagine what would be the results if a seller were to use these openings. He, therefore, has to take great care to plan in advance what he is going to say, so ensuring that there is no risk of antagonising anyone. His objective is to make sure that all the operators are well sold on the equipment, so that when new orders are placed they will speak highly of the equipment.

The seller could use any of the standard openings – asking a question, or stating a fact:

> 'Do any of you find difficulty in using the threaded . . .?'
> 'I have found on some calls that operators have not been told initially that by using the barlock at No.10 frequency there is no risk of . . .'

In neither of these openings does he risk upsetting the operators, and he is using exactly the same *form* of opening as he would use if his objective was selling the equipment, instead of calling back to maintain goodwill and increase product knowledge.

2. *To get an introduction to another buyer.*

In exactly the same way as if he were selling, the salesperson would plan how to phrase the opening sentence. He might ask a question:

'Mr Brown, do you know if Mr Kenton in your S Division uses block struts as you do here?'

'I'm not certain.'

'Then would you mind introducing me to him so that I can see if we can be as helpful to his division as we always try to be to yours?'

3. *To discover the real reason why a competitor is obtaining business (buyers rarely give the real reason for changing).*

To achieve this objective can be difficult. Would it be achieved by trying to wheedle the information out of an employee? Surely this form of ferreting out information borders on the unethical. The sales agent might, therefore, decide to use a Fact-plus-Question Opening when talking to a friendly employee:

'John, as you know we supply over 60 per cent of the Cyclatones in the British Isles and that percentage increases every year. But we still don't want to lose any of it. Can you tell me, therefore, if there is any reason why Mrs Johnson, your buyer, has decided to use Cyclatones supplied by XYZ?'

Most people will react to a direct question, and John will probably be no different from others.

Although the objectives of a seller may be varied and may cover a wide area, the majority call to negotiate or obtain orders.

Sometimes a seller can call on a buyer twenty times or more, attempting to open the account. Salespeople supplying customers with component parts may call every four weeks on a buyer; others may call two or three times a year,

BUT

following the *chat gap*, a seller must still obtain the undivided attention of the buyer – assistant buyer – research and development manager – accountant . . . whoever it is whose mind the salesperson has to influence.

Every seller, at every call, must have an objective, and on that objective will be based the opening technique he will use. Without an objective a seller risks using a colourless, cliché-ridden opening, which makes it so easy for a buyer to end the interview quickly.

Here are examples of weak call-back openings:

- 'Any news for me?'
- 'Have you heard from the Board yet?'
- 'Have you had a chance yet of discussing the matter with the contractors?'
- 'I hope you have some good news for me today.'
- 'Have you arrived at a decision yet?'
- 'Were you able to check the stock?'

Following this type of weak opening, it is so easy for a buyer to reply negatively: 'No, the Board hasn't yet decided'; 'No, I haven't studied the quotation yet; 'No, I haven't had the stock checked since you last called; come back again in four weeks' time . . .'

As much care must be taken with a Call-back Opening as with a first call. All of the standard techniques can be used when calling back.

Here are some examples:

Factual Opening:

'Because of the world shortage of Salycotes we shall

shortly be changing to a synthetic. I felt sure you would want to place a large order now, while the Salycotes are still available . . .'

Factual Opening:

'Ms Smith, you are using approximately 120,000 metres of Dylet a month. An analysis of your orders over the past year shows a steady growth, which means that within three months you will be needing 150,000 metres regularly. Deliveries are getting tighter and I don't want to let you down so if you order now . . .'

*   *   *

Both of these openings can lead to a quick close:

Question Opening:

'The trend seems to be to switch from business class to economy class. How is that going to affect your travel policy?'
'It could cause problems.'
'Well, here is a way we can help you . . .'

Question Opening:

'How are you being affected by the skills shortage in this area, Mr Jones?'
'It's getting worse every day.'
'Here is a way we can help you: since I last called we have devised a system which will save you . . .'

*   *   *

Reference Opening:

'I called on your friend Brian Walker yesterday. He suggested that I should tell you about the results he is getting with Gripit. You haven't used it for some time now, Miss

Brown, but I am sure you will want to consider it . . .'

* * *

Sales Aid Opening:

'I have brought you our latest catalogue, Mr Lyons. It now gives a complete range of spare parts, which is in line with the suggestion you made a year ago. I'd like to show you . . .'

* * *

When a seller calls regularly on retail/wholesale customers he should dispense with stock phrases such as:

'How are you?'
'Has the stock been moving?'
'Is trade any better?'
'Were the goods delivered on time?'
'Did the display arrive?'
'Anything for me today?'

These are time-wasters. No matter how frequently a seller sees a customer he can find something new to say about his products. Before each visit he should decide on a factual sentence, or a question, or a term of reference that will put fresh life into the sale. For example:

'Good morning, Ms Jones. When I was here last month I told you about our new advertising campaign. I have some facts for you now which should help you to decide on your stock requirements.'

'Good morning, Mr Smith. Have you noticed that over the past five weeks there has been a sudden demand for reds and greens? We have added some variations of these colours to our range.'

'Mr Brown, after I left you last time I thought of an idea which would help you to sell more of . . .'

'Good morning, Mrs Green. I must apologise to you.

When I was here five weeks ago I didn't really explain in detail what a tie-up with our promotional campaign means. But you will remember that you were very busy at the time. Do forgive me – this is how it can help you . . .'

The order-takers use hackneyed approaches. The professional salesperson thinks of something new at every call.

Most salespeople use the factual, question, or reference approach. These additional forms of approach can, however, be used occasionally:

The Curiosity Approach:

'Good morning, Ms Green. Have you ever seen a printer like this before? It can save you a lot of money. It is an accessory used in our new . . .'

The Fear Approach:

'Mr Jones, what would happen to your house if a fire bloke out while you and your children were asleep in bed? Our fire alarm . . .'

The Gift Approach:

'Mr Smith? Good morning, will you please accept this CD with our compliments? We want you to try it and I also want to show you . . .'

The Personal Interest Approach:

'Good morning, Miss Brown. I was very interested to read your excellent letter in this morning's *Telegraph*. Every statement you made was quite right, but naturally, I was sorry to hear of the bad service you had received from the X Car Company. This need never happen to you again. I am from the ABC Garages. We are sole distributors in the area for Y cars, and I have called to ask you to let us show you a model of . . .'

THE LINK OPENING

Thriller serials on television make regular use of the technique of showing a flashback from the final scene of the previous episode. It is this link with the past which immediately involves the viewer in the new episode.

The *Link Opening* in selling uses the same technique as the flashback on TV. A point discussed at one call becomes the link to hold the buyer's attention at the beginning of the next call.

Although the link technique can be used whatever the objective of the call back, it is most useful to those industrial sales agents whose products are repeatable and who, therefore, call on their buyers every four to six weeks, year in and year out.

'What can I say that is new,' they ask, 'when we have nothing exciting to offer for periods of six or nine months, or more?'

To these salespeople, the *link* helps maintain a continuing dialogue, the seller probing, questioning, reminding, with the objective of selling strongly at every call to get the maximum business *at every call*. Sometimes only a few words are needed – words most pleasing to a buyer: 'You will remember when last I called you said . . .' We are all anxious to hear our words of wisdom repeated.

If this link is not feasible, the seller can refer to a question left unanswered, a statement made by a third party, or a point made previously in which the buyer has shown interest.

For example:

> 'Mrs Jones, you will remember last month you said that the problem of off-cuts was becoming acute. I have been thinking very deeply about this point, and I want to suggest that . . .'
>
> 'Mr Smith, when I was here last week you told me of your plan to . . . This is how we can help your plan along . . .'
>
> 'Mr White, when I brought in your quotation last week I showed you the drawings, but forgot to mention . . .'

There is one DON'T that every salesperson should remember when working out a *Link Opening*. If, at a previous call, you have dealt with a complaint and settled that complaint, DON'T bring the matter up again by saying, 'Is the machine working all right now?' This will begin a trend of negative thoughts in the buyer's mind. If anything is wrong he will tell you, quickly enough.

Always recall *positive* points:

> 'Mr Johnson, last month you told me that it was essential for you to have the motors by the 24th. Well, they left for the site yesterday, the 17th. As I promised, I was determined to give your order priority. But, Mr Johnson, deliveries will get progressively worse, and I feel sure that you will now want to . . .'

> 'I really appreciated the confidence you showed in me when I called last month and you told me of what was happening. *The Times* only published the news yesterday, but those three weeks have enabled us to draw up a new plan for you . . .'

> 'There was one point we touched on last week, Mrs Brown, when I called, and that was the noise factor. You said you were going to look into the question and, of course, with embossing machines the noise can, sometimes, be deafening. Now with our machines there is less noise than that of a computer . . .'

> 'Mr Bright, when I was here last week I promised to bring you a photograph of some of our conference rooms, to give you some indication of how our experience can help you. I have had this photograph taken specially for you . . .'

GETTING ATTENTION

1. Never sell under adverse conditions.
2. Don't gabble; always speak slowly so that the buyer can hear every word.
3. Keep the *chat gap* as short as possible.
4. Make certain that you have worked out the best possible opening sentence, based on:
   (a) Factual Opening
   (b) Question Opening
   (c) Reference Opening
   (d) Sales Aid Opening
   (e) Demonstration Opening
5. When calling back, make sure that you get attention by using any of the standard openings, or a Link Opening.
6. Always remember, the objective of the opening is to obtain the undivided attention of the buyer.

11

Offer Analysis

Thomas Carlisle wrote: *Let him who would move and convince others be first moved to convince himself.*

A seller must be able to prove for himself that he is selling the right product, and offer analysis provides that proof, enabling him to identify *all* product features, and derive from them every single buyer benefit. It is the accumulation of these benefits which give proof of the value of the product.

To analyse, the dictionary informs us, is:

> *To take to pieces; to resolve into constituent elements; to examine minutely; to examine critically.*

To be able to offer a buyer every conceivable benefit, a salesperson rarely has to take his product to pieces, but he will certainly have to examine it minutely, and critically.

It isn't enough to analyse a product alone. The analysis must be complete, and embrace every factor which could influence a favourable decision.

For example, what will create buyer confidence?

A buyer cannot see, in advance of purchasing, honesty – a fair deal – the backing given to a guarantee (what is a guarantee worth if a company goes bankrupt?) – completion of work on time – advertising campaigns – help during periods of shortages – store promotions – rapid service . . . Unless a customer believes that some or all of these assets exist, he may decide to buy from one of his regular suppliers.

The Small Company

The seller joining a newly formed or small company will soon appreciate the need for confidence builders. Prospects may voice their fears by saying, 'Where are these in use? We have to be assured of continuity of supplies' or, 'I am not opening any new accounts.'

To overcome these fears of being let down on deliveries, of quality not being up to samples submitted, of costly replacements, the sales offer must include confidence-building sentences based on company analysis like:

- 'Our company has been established only about twelve months, but our managing director was, for twenty years, chief engineer with the largest electronics firm in America. It is his vast experience that has developed . . .'
- 'We are only a small company, Miss Brown, but we are local. That means that you will get prompt and personal service, not only from me but also from our managing director.'
- 'Because we are fairly small, we operate only in a limited area. This keeps our costs down and we can pass the benefit on to you.'

The Larger Company

Sales staff employed by a large organisation sometimes believe that the good reputation of their company ensures the confidence of its customers for ever. This might be true if there were no competitors – which is a rare occurrence.

A seller working for a market leader should still evolve confidence-building sentences:

'We spend nearly three-quarters of a million a year on research, and you receive the benefit. Of course, the time will come when smaller companies will copy us, but by then we shall be even further ahead.'

'There is no special merit in being large, but we have grown so rapidly because we are efficient. We always strive to improve service for our customers, and we even give it at a loss, if necessary.' (The inference here is that a smaller company could not afford losses.)

'Because of our wide ramifications, Mr Brown, we can

offer you a free survey. Our electronics engineer will come down here and evaluate . . .'

'The very size of our company enables us to give you a very special service. We have depots near all of your branches; we keep stocks high to guarantee you immediate delivery; and when we assure you that we are going to spend £250,000 on an advertising campaign, you know that we won't spend a penny less.' (The inference here is that a small company may not always be able to keep its promises.)

Every seller indirectly criticises competitors' products, so every seller must build confidence to refute the implied criticism. Although a customer may have dealt with an agent for many years, he must still be constantly reminded of the main reasons for the company's high reputation.

Here are sentences which project the right image of a company:

'May I arrange for you to visit our new factory? It is one of the most up-to-date production units in the country, and it would help you to impress upon *your* customers the value they are buying.'

'Our company is sixty years old this month, but I know you will agree that it is very young in its outlook, always trying for better quality, better value.'

Whether a company is large or small, there is always some aspect of its background which can be turned into a confidence builder.

Even before analysing a product or service, a seller should ask himself, *Why should a buyer have confidence in my company?* Surely not because of a claim to be the longest established, or the largest. Old-established may be a euphemism for old-fashioned. One pictures a series of medals on a company's headed notepaper – relics of exhibition awards in 1897 – and then one thinks of an obsolete plant, self-perpetuating directors, nepotism . . .

We are the largest can mean a newly acquired member of a huge conglomerate, and conglomerates are only as good as the management teams of their diversified companies.

To discover true customer benefits, the seller must use the questioning technique, but the questions should be related not only to the product, but the total ramifications of a company. Every fact, every feature must be analysed and the resulting benefits incorporated into the sales offer. This is the reason for this chapter being called *Offer Analysis* and not Product Analysis.

Here are examples of the types of questions which could be asked:

- What is special about our factory?
- Do we use machinery that allows for better quality – finish – durability?
- Do our management team have special qualifications? (For example, our managing director is a technical adviser to a Government department – our research chemists have developed a substance of world-wide renown.)
- Do localised depots help speed deliveries?
- In what way does our research and development team help our customers?
- In what way do our exports help the home market?
- How will the packing of our products help our customers?
- How does our service department offer a better service than our competitors?

The objective of Offer Analysis is to identify and list every product feature, company advantage, advertising and promotional scheme, assets of company personnel, and then turn these features into benefits for the buyer.

Be Selective

A complete analysis may result in the listing of a hundred or more features leading to two hundred benefits. This is unusual, but it can happen, for example, when an agent carries a wide range of component parts. However, most product analysis results in approximately ten features, twenty general benefits and perhaps thirty selective, or personal benefits.

In many sales interviews, a salesperson can give his total sales offer, while at others he should be selective.

The complete analysis provides a salesperson with a storehouse of features/benefits from which he can select those applicable to the buyer he is facing. The more thorough and complete the analysis, the better the seller is able to select benefits which will motivate a buyer.

Another reason for the essential need of a complete analysis is to enable a salesperson to evolve *double benefits*.

If the agent is selling to a retailer or a wholesaler or is calling on an architect, consulting engineer, or any authority, the 'buyer' is concerned with the needs of his clients/customers. He has to be sure that he is giving the best advice, that standards will be maintained, or that his customer will benefit from buying from him. In the sales offer, a sellern calling on a retailer will incorporate in his offer a benefit to the buyer *and* his client.

Beating Competition

Imagine now that you are selling a device used in the manufacture of a domestic appliance. This device, incorporating a special unit with a five-point control, allows the manufacturer to work to fine limits.

You decide that it is hardly worthwhile incorporating this feature in your sales offer because all three of your competitors, A, B and C, also have five-point controls on their devices. But the salesperson of Company B does stress this well-known feature – and gets the order, the buyer being under the impression that B's device is different, and has an additional advantage of a five-point control, while others may only have a three- or four-point control.

The buyer is only under this misapprehension because neither you nor the salespeople from A or C companies had thought it worthwhile telling him about it.

Remember, then, when working out your sales offer, do not leave out features/benefits which are taken for granted. Buyers are rarely as knowledgeable as they would like salespeople to believe. Always incorporate in your offer *standard* benefits, even if they can be claimed by competitors.

Now you might ask this question:

> *What happens when all competitors carefully work out their sales offers, when we all give similar benefits; who will then get the orders?*

Firstly, remember that when all things are equal the orders are generally placed with the seller a buyer likes and trusts the most. Secondly, it depends on your ability to find that *extra* benefit.

Picture now a pair of jockey scales with the buyer occupying the jockey's seat and you replacing the weights. The buyer is listening to your sales offer and considering whether he should buy from you or not.

Through his mind runs these thoughts:

> *Could I buy better elsewhere?*
> *Can I get a better price?*
> *Can I depend on deliveries?*
> *Can I rely on what this salesperson is promising?*
> *Will it break down?*
> *Will they be able to give immediate after-sales service?*
> *I don't think their locking device is as good as the one I saw last week.*
> *I'd be safer to rely on Company B – I know them well.*
> *I'd better think it over.*

All the time he is weighing up the proposal, the weight of his negative thoughts depress his side of the scale. The odds move against your getting an order.

Then you begin to build strong benefits, and gradually the scale moves slightly in your favour. Eventually, to your great relief, as you add benefit upon benefit, your scale moves sharply down and the buyer's moves upwards.

At the tenth benefit, the scales are equally poised. It is the moment of decision, but still the buyer hesitates – and, while he is undecided, you add one more benefit. It might be only of marginal importance – almost gossamer-light in weight: *The second-hand value remains high, Mr Brown. In five years' time, we can offer you . . .'*

Your offer might be of small moment to the buyer, but it is fractionally more than the figure suggested by a competitor –

although insignificant compared to the total offer. To your delight, you hear the buyer saying, 'Perhaps it will do the job – the order is yours.'

The scale has been tilted only slightly – so slightly – in your favour, but it is enough.

We have been told by salespeople that they have often remembered this story when the going was hard, and it reminded them *always* to look for that extra benefit to beat the competition.

Now you might ask,

> 'But if I've worked hard on the offer analysis, how can I possibly find an *extra* benefit?'

There is always one extra benefit. The effort to find it is worthwhile. Imagine your life depended on squeezing an orange dry with your hands. You are handed a medium-sized orange and told that if one drop of juice is left, your life will be forfeit. So you begin to squeeze, relax, squeeze again, relax, apply more pressure, and squeeze even harder. Finally, with aching hands and tired muscles, you believe you have succeeded – you feel safe. Looking down at the inert, misshapen, dry mass of useless pulp you hear the voice of the executioner saying, 'It is not enough.' With fear sapping your strength, you make a final, determined effort. You squeeze, squeeze again. Nothing happens. You take a deep breath and exert every ounce of pressure . . . One more drop of juice slowly drips from the pulp.

Squeezing the orange has a message for all industrial agents. Your livelihood and an important order could depend on your ability to *squeeze* that extra benefit from the product. To do this, you must think again of buying motivation – rational and emotional reasons why people buy, checking each feature again against each motivator. You may have overlooked the emotional appeal of pride, the rational appeal of security, or some tiny aspect in the history of your company which will give additional confidence to the buyer. You must find that extra benefit.

Telling Isn't Selling

Many industrial sales agents use words, sentences and expressions, and make statements, which apparently offer benefits but
have no impact on the buyer. For example:

> *It will increase your profit.*
> *It will do a marvellous job.*
> *It is self-cleaning.*
> *Everyone is delighted with the results.*
> *We can deliver them right away.*
> *Our service is first-class.*
> *They are sold all over the world.*

There are hundreds of these superlatives which sound so fine
to the salesperson, but factual statements do not personalise a
benefit, and it is personal benefits which motivate a buyer.

Salespeople, therefore, need a constant reminder to explain
benefits in terms of the buyers' interests.

You will never forget to personalise benefits if you will always
remember these three link words:

> *which means that*

They are sold all over the world is a confidence-building sentence
used by many salespeople. By adding the words *which means that* it
can be considerably strengthened:

> 'They are sold all over the world, *which means that* your
> agents can get immediate service.'

We *maintain huge stocks*. What does that mean? How huge are
the stocks? The word *huge* can be interpreted differently by
different people. How much stronger when a seller says:

> 'We maintain huge stocks, *which means that* we can almost
> take over your inventory problems, and like others of our
> customers, you will cut down on stocks by 30 per cent or
> more because we deliver so quickly.'

By using the words *which means that*, you will be certain to give
the benefit 'YOU' appeal. The YOU is, of course, the buyer.

Every sale must have YOU appeal.

Here are many instances from some of the varied companies using this TACK formula:

Sketchley Ltd – Sketchley Overall Services

'Ours is a complete service, *which means that* we take over all the problems of having stocks of the right size and type to satisfy you and your employees.'

Pinchin Johnson & Associates Ltd – Decorative Paint Division

'This aluminium paint incorporates highly polished leafing aluminium in a silicone medium and will be unaffected by heats of up to 1,000°F, *which means that* if this material is used on your exhaust stacks, their appearance will be maintained for a much longer time than with conventional paints.'

Spillers Ltd – Animal Feed

'Our Calf Cudlets have been designed to replace a whole milk diet via early weaning, *which means that* the calf can be reared more cheaply, with less labour, and with reduced incidence of nutritional upset.'

L. M. Van Moppes & Sons (Diamond Tools) Ltd

'This is a new design in diamond wheel-dressing tools. Its purchase price is much in line with ordinary-price dressers. It is, however, intended to be used to destruction without the necessity of resetting, *which means that* fewer tools need to be stocked to cover the resetting time, and also the machine operator spends less time changing the diamond.'

Drake & Fletcher Ltd – Engineers

'The centrifugal fan used only on Victair sprayers is far quieter than all competitive types of sprayer, *which means that* there is far less fatigue for the operator.'

Yardley & Co Ltd – Perfumiers and Fine Soap Makers

'You will see that our talcum powder is packed in a new

plastic container. It is light and easy to handle, unbreakable and rust-proof, *which means that* the true fragrance of the talc is preserved for much longer than if any other form of packaging were used.'

Blick Time Recorders Ltd

'This is a Blick fully automatic, one-hand-operated electric card-system time-recorder, printing lateness and overtime in red for rapid analysis in your accounts department, *which means that* there is no time wasted. Staff clock in and out without delays or fumbling; they just put the card in the machine, and the rest is automatic.'

I. & R. Morley Ltd – Hosiery Manufacturers

'This underwear is made from fabric knitted in such a way that it produces efficient insulating properties, *which means that* the garment is suitable for both summer and winter.'

Slazengers Ltd – Sports Goods Manufacturers

'In the old days, tennis balls started smooth and wore even smoother, so that control in play was much more difficult. The Slazenger tennis hall is covered with a specially developed cloth called TW or tennis weave – a combination of wool and nylon – *which means that* it will wear in new-ball condition for hours of play.'

Lansing Bagnall Ltd – Fork Trucks and Towtractor Manufacturers

'With this truck, you will reduce your gangways to six feet, *which means that* you will store 20 per cent more material in this warehouse.'

Here is an example of how a seller can begin to work out his feature/benefit/YOU appeal for a specific type of fork-lift truck:

Features: uses diesel oil or LP gas
Benefits no need to recharge battery
no need for battery replacements
no depending on electrical means for recharging

batteries gives maximum performance all the time

These are all the facts derived from only one feature of the fork-lift truck. There could, of course, be many more.

Now let us give these facts YOU appeal:

YOU Appeal
1. No need for recharging batteries, which means that YOU will increase the work load without increasing costs. That is quite a saving . . .
2. No need for battery replacements, which means that YOU will cut costs.
3. YOU will not be dependent on electric mains for recharging the batteries, which means that your drivers will not have to waste time moving away to an electrical junction or running a cable. The truck can be used anywhere at any time – a huge advantage in a very busy factory like yours.
4. YOU will get maximum performance all the time, which means that the running costs are cheaper.

Offer Analysis Sheet
To achieve the objectives of listing features/benefits/YOU appeal and remembering *which means that*, a simple device can be used: an Offer Analysis sheet. This sheet helps you to organise your knowledge of your product or service in such a way that it becomes easy to link features to benefits and then express these as personal benefits, with the relevant YOU appeal.

As many sheets as necessary may be used. The following examples are copies of Offer Analysis sheets completed by delegates attending our courses:

OFFER ANALYSIS SHEET
Product or Services: Car radio aerials

FEATURES	BENEFITS	*which means that*	'YOU' APPEAL
Wide range of *high-quality* aerials.	1. Fewer returns or complaints. 2. Looks much better on car. 3. Wider range of customers.		1. You have more time to deal with profitable work. . 2. Your customer will be pleased with your recommendation. 3. You increase your turnover.
Made at our modern factory with its own delivery vans.	1. Faster and better deliveries. 2. Any problems more easily settled. 3. No need to carry large stock.		1. You know the goods will arrive on time allowing you to give a better service to your customer. 2. You can save time and worry. 3. You don't have a large capital outlay.
Special bulk packing.	1. More storage space. 2. Easier to handle. 3. Cheaper to buy in bulk.		1. You can hold a larger range of stocks. 2. You save time in moving goods. 3. You save money and increase your profits.
Six-section rod-set incorporating lantern-springing between each section.	1. Short underhang. 2. Longer rod-set. 3. Greater stability, will not sway about causing distraction, even at high speeds.		1. You can assure your customer that it will fit easily on cars with limited under-wing space. 2. It will give better reception in difficult areas, therefore helping you to close more sales. 3. Your customer can tune radio in more easily and quickly.

Continued on next page

OFFER ANALYSIS SHEET
Product or Services: Car radio aerials

FEATURES	BENEFITS	which means that	'YOU' APPEAL
Stainless steel, fully retractable lock-down aerial.	1. Rod-set rust-proof.		1. You can offer your customer a long-term, more economical product.
	2. High-quality prestige material.		2. Your fitters will experience the satisfaction and pride of good workmanship.
	3. Collapses completely into the wing of the car, allowing the utility of automatic car-washes.		3. You do not lose customer-goodwill by advising the purchase of an aerial which could be subsequently irrevocably damaged during a car-wash.
	4. Locks down safe from vandals.		4. You can give your customer a built-in safety device to save him expense.
42° angled zinc-plated saddle with earthing teeth.	1. Will not rust.		1. Giving your customer permanent earthing system, saving expensive returns.
	2. Teeth clamp through under-seal.		2. Saving your fitters time-consuming job of scraping away unwanted insulation (underseal, etc.).
	3. Will fit entirely from the top of the car wing.		3. No need for your fitters to remove wheel-arch splash-covers.
	4. Strengthened material.		4. Cannot be split by over-tightening, saving you extra expense on occasion.
Polypropylene-injected body housing.	1. Will not rust from under-wing spray, stopping interference.		1. You save money by reducing expensive guarantee claims.
	2. Waterproof.		2. Saves the risk of shorting-out when raining, perhaps causing you unnecessary complaints.

5 ft low-loss, high-density, braid-coaxial cable with split.	1. No need for extra length of cable to be supplied. 2. Eliminates interference. 3. Rubber grommet protects cable from being cut by tough edges of drilled holes. 4. Grommet split to enable fitting needed after aerial fitting is completed.	1. Saving you time from lengthy route calculations. 2. Less engine-suppression needed – less work for your fitters. 3. As it stops short-circuiting you save on eventual replacements when your time could be used more profitably. 4. Saves your fitter frustration and time if forgotten due to haste or through distraction.
Uniquely designed plug.	1. No fish-hooks. 2. Securely fixed to outer core of cable. 3. Fully sprung around outer edge. 4. Insulated inside.	1. It can be removed easily if incorrect route selected. 2. It cannot be pulled off under pressure, causing time-wasting for your fitters. 3. There will be a fine contact which will not fall out. 4. Avoids you checking the whole installation for an interference fault which may not be apparent.

OFFER ANALYSIS SHEET
Product or Services: Tiles (peel and stick)

FEATURES	BENEFITS	*which means that*	'YOU' APPEAL
Wide range of colours.	1. Bright appearance.		1. You attract customer attention by enhancing shop/store display.
	2. Eye-catching.		2. Passers-by will stop at your windows.
	3. Pleases a variety of tastes in colour.		3. You have a greater opportunity to increase sales.
	4. Colours suitable for all bathrooms, kitchens, halls, passages, etc.		4. You can profit by increasing sales for a variety of areas.
Peel and stick.	1. Easy to lay.		1. Sales are easier because your customer needs no special knowledge or qualifications.
	2. Adhesive already applied to tile.		2. Your customer becomes instantly interested and buys quicker.
	3. Measured application of adhesive.		3. You will have no complaints from customers who might apply too much or too little adhesive as with some other tiles, saving you wasting time on such complaints.
Well packaged.	1. Easy handling.		1. You profit from time-saving.
	2. Laying instructions on package.		2. Your customer gains confidence from learning of the simplicity of laying the tiles.
	3. Good presentation.		3. Your customer is impressed with the value you are offering.

		4. You can calculate the number of packs required easily and quickly, resulting in a more rapid closing of the sale.
	4. One-square-yard package.	
Display stand.	1. Easy stock control.	1. You can maintain stocks at correct level, satisfying all customers without risking over-stocking.
	2. Compact	2. You use available space to the maximum benefit.
	3. Neat appearance.	3. Your customer is encouraged to buy.
	4. Free.	4. You have no need to spend money building shelves, etc.
Made of vinyl.	1. Non-absorbent.	1. Your customer has no cleaning problems.
	2. Tough and resilient.	2. Your customer is satisfied by its wearing qualities and will recommend your shop to friends.
	3. Will not crack, rot, or decay.	3. Your customer will have no maintenance problems, or complaints to you about bad wear.
	4. Clear vinyl coating.	4. Because there is no deterioration in appearance, your customers will always be reminded of the good advice you gave.
Brochure.	1. Aids sale.	1. You can give a brochure to a prospective customer, knowing that it will help to convince that customer to return to you and buy.
	2. Colourful.	2. Your display is brightened.
	3. Shows a floor design-chart.	3. Your customer is intrigued and is helped, making closing sales easier for you.

OFFER ANALYSIS SHEET
Product or Services: PVC Synthetic Veneers

FEATURES	BENEFITS	*which means that*	'YOU' APPEAL
Company has large Research and Development Department	1. Full technical data provided.		1. You can ensure that the material meets your technical standards.
	2. Advice on technical matters.		2. You can call on our vast experiences to help you solve problems.
	3. New and improved products are continually being looked at.		3. You can be confident that you have the best possible product available.
Laminating.	1. *Laminated* equipment and adhesives can be recommended.		1. As you take the minimum time finding suitable manufacturers, you save time and money.
Wide range of wood-grain designs and effects available.	1. Most natural wood-veneers can be matched from our range.		1. You are able to offer your own customers an equally wide choice, thus increasing sales.
	2. All types of furniture, caravan interiors, and wall-boards can be produced.		2. You can increase the market for your products, so increasing your profits.
	3. Current trends and fashions are catered for.		3. You can maintain and increase sales despite your customers' design variations.
	4. Varied tastes catered for.		4. You will increase turnover by adding to your sales outlets.
Available in long, wide rolls.	1. Cuts down time.		1. You get higher output.
	2. High-speed laminating can be achieved.		2. You get maximum possible production.
	3. Fully automatic laminating equipment can be used.		3. Your labour costs are kept to a minimum.

Print protected finish.	1. No further processing needed. 2. Durable finished surface. 3. Resistant to staining.	1. Your manufacturing costs are reduced. 2. You won't have the danger of damage during transit to your customer. 3. You can use this material on a wide range of products.
Supplied in final colours and finish to individual customer's specification.	1. Ensures product suitability. 2. Can be matched to existing products. 3. No colour variation from batch to batch.	1. You have the best possible product for the job. 2. You can offer a full and comprehensive range. 3. You can supply unit furniture over several years and your customers can be confident that the units will match.
Sample stocks of each design available.	1. Initial product test-marketing can be carried out. 2. Immediate delivery. 3. Material can be fully evaluated under production conditions. 4. Substrates and adhesives can be evaluated at the same time as the PVC.	1. You can obtain market reaction to your product for a small outlay. 2. You can produce and provide a quick sampling service to your customers. 3. You can easily work out costings and price levels. 4. You save time and money.

OFFER ANALYSIS SHEET

Product or Services: Cigarette lighters

FEATURES	BENEFITS	*which means that*	'YOU' APPEAL	
			RETAILER	CONSUMER
Famous name printed on lighter.	1. A sign that every lighter is backed by an international company of the highest repute.		1. You can create confidence, quickly resulting in time-saving as sales are more easily closed.	1. They will be proud to posses a lighter with such a famous name. They will have no worry about giving a lighter with such a name to someone whose respect is valued.
	2. Experience in manufacturing lighters is unrivalled.		2. Your turnover will increase because our reputation is so high in the lighter field.	2. They will know that you are giving the best possible advice.
	3. The name is synonymous with quality-controlled manufacture.		3. You will profit from not having to waste time on unnecessary complaints.	3. They will always appreciate that you sold a lighter which needs so little service.
They are pocket size.	1. Because they take up little space, they are ideal for display. High value/space ratio.		1. You can benefit from excellent shop or window displays which, although taking up little space, attract customer attention.	

	2. Complete stocks can be carried in the minimum of space. 3. Can be sold as men's or women's lighters.	2. You can benefit by carrying wide range, thus offering a selection which will increase sales. 3. You can reduce overall stocks.	2. Customer will appreciate the selection you can offer. 3. Both men and women will appreciate that the lighter fits snugly into either a pocket or the smallest handbag.
Special flame adjustment.	1. Will light pipes or cigarettes with equal ease. 2. With flame set high, will light in high wind.	1. You can satisfy both categories of smoker and increase turnover.	1. Delighted and proud to show the benefits of an all-purpose lighter which can be used in nearly all environments.
Precision-engineered vents.	1. Exact assembly of product to produce optimum functional capability.	1. When you demonstrate the lighter you will know that it will operate at once in nine flicks out of ten – this advantage must result in increased sales.	1. Everyone will appreciate the lighter's reliability.

Continued on next page

OFFER ANALYSIS SHEET
Product or Services: Cigarette lighters

FEATURES	BENEFITS	*which means that*	'YOU' APPEAL	
			RETAILER	CONSUMER
Highly efficient after-sales service, including one year's guarantee.	1. Rapid return of any faulty lighter.		1. If a lighter should be defective you will keep your customer's goodwill by the speedy service you can offer.	1. They will benefit from an efficient and speedy service not always obtainable from foreign lighters.
	2. No need for customer to waste time attempting to repair a lighter.		2. At the initial sales you will sell the lighters quickly as you and the customers will know you are selling a guaranteed product.	2. Their sense of caution is satisfied by purchasing a guaranteed lighter – a guarantee that really means something.
	3. Spares always available.		3. You will benefit from the sale of genuine spare-parts.	
Spring-loaded positive lighting.	1. Lighter cannot light accidentally in pocket.		1. You will quickly secure customers' interest by pin-pointing safety factor.	1. No worry about danger of lighter igniting in handbag or pocket.
	2. Adds to the appearance of lighter.		2. Because most people are motivated by appearance, you will be able to close sales quickly.	2. They will be proud to show the lighter to others.
	3. Easy action.		3. This will help you to give impact to the demonstration.	3. The easy action will appeal to men and especially to women.

| Chromed metal-alloy casing. | 1. Exceptionally good appearance.
2. Easy to keep clean.
3. Not easily damaged or scratched.
4. Durable.
5. No danger of puncturing gas tank.
6. Light in weight. | 1. You will be able to gain customers' immediate attention.
2. You will not have to waste time cleaning lighters when they are on display.
3. There is less chance of their becoming shop-soiled.
4. You can explain more easily the long-term value of the purchase.
5. You will be able to emphasise this safety factor and close the sale more readily.
6. You can let the customer test for himself that it will not feel heavy in his pocket. | 1. They will be proud of having such a lighter.
2. They will know that the lighter will retain its appearance.
3. They will not have to polish the lighter continually to keep its appearance.
4. They will save money because the lighter is so durable.
5. They will not be afraid of subsequent damage to pocket or handbag.
6. They will be delighted at ease of handling. |
| Gas. | 1. Clean.
2. No evaporation.
3. Simple refuelling. | 1. Profitable gas releases.
2. No flooding – always works on demonstration.
3. Ronson refills obtainable all round the world. | 1. No smell.
2. Instant use even after a long 'lay-off'.
3. Only a few seconds needed about once a month. |

OFFER ANALYSIS SHEET

Product or Services: Blister pack needles

FEATURES	BENEFITS	*which means that*	'YOU' APPEAL
Made of finest steel.	1. They last longer.		1. You are selling to your customers a needle that will last, thus keeping their goodwill and recommendations.
Presentation on plastic.	1. Neatly separated needles.		1. A sale is readily made because your customers, when sewing, can easily choose the needles they need.
	2. Plastic is hard-wearing.		2. You have an additional sales point. Your customers can use the holder over and over again without breakage.
	3. It is attractive.		3. Eye-appeal can make and close a sale quickly – saving your time.
Bright red pack.	1. Easy to see.		1. Your customers will ask for these needles because the pack will catch their eye.
Strong cardboard pack.	1. Retains its appearance.		1. It will be openly used by your customers over a long period of time – a constant reminder of your service.
	2. Holds needles together firmly.		2. Your customer is less likely to lose them. A strong selling point for your assistant.
	3. It is re-usable.		3. You can demonstrate the pack over and over again.
	4. It is attractive.		4. Eye-appeal can make and close a sale quickly – saving you time.

See-through plastic front.	1. The needles can be seen. 2. The needles can be counted.	1. Your customers can choose their needle before they open the packet. 2. You can show your customers the value they are getting for their money.
Easy opening and folding back.	1. It is quick to use. 2. It is self-closing. 3. It is easy to demonstrate.	1. You lose less time selling with this pack. 2. You don't have to fiddle with a fastener. 3. You save time selling.
The special complete package.	1. Increased sales.	1. Your turnover in needles will increase, resulting in operator-profitability to you.

163

OFFER ANALYSIS SHEET

Product or Services: Prefabricated cubicles

FEATURES	BENEFITS	*which means that*	'YOU' APPEAL
Purpose-made services.	1. Flexibility of layout.		1. You reduce design costs. You reduced building costs. You save space.
	2. Flexibility of designs.		2. You can make more efficient use of space. Your particular requirements catered for. You do not incur excessive 'specials' prices. You can use for a wider range of applications.
	3. Change of construction offered.		3. You have a choice to suit your needs.
	4. Range of finishes and colours.		4. You can select to harmonise with any colour scheme.
Manufactured from mela- mine-faced chipboard or WBP plywood.	1. Economic material.		1. You reduce prime costs.
	2. High strength/weight ratio.		2. You benefit from reduced transfer costs. You benefit from low erection costs. You benefit from quickness of erection time.
	3. Hard-wearing surface.		3. You save on maintenance costs. You save on cleaning costs.
	4. Permanent colour.		4. You avoid redecorating costs.
	5. Hygienic finish.		5. You save on cleaning and disinfecting costs.
	6. Available as separate panels.		6. You can use same material for other associated structures to obtain matching installations, e.g., duct covers, etc.

Supplied in kit form.	1. Allows convenient and easy packing. 2. Easier to apply protective packing. 3. Simplicity of erection and fittings. 4. Ease of site-handling. 5. Minimum number of fittings and pre-packed. 6. Minimum bulk.	1. You benefit from reduced transport costs. You gain quicker delivery by reducing transport time. 2. You experience less delays and costs due to damage in transit or on site. 3. Your erection times and costs reduce. You require less-skilled labour. 4. You reduce erection and labour costs. You reduce risk of site damage. You reduce time of erection. 5. You minimise delays and costs through site-pilferage and loss. 6. You benefit from reduced transport costs. You achieve less inconvenience in storing on site. You need only minimum storage space on site. You have less risk of damage on site. You require less protection on site.
Metal-faced chipboard or WBP plywood.	1. Durable finish. 2. Textured surface available. 3. Suitable base for good paint finish. 4. Non-rust surfaces available. 5. Allows quick and easy repairs.	1. You reduce damage by harsh use or vandalism. 2. You minimise writing or defacing. 3. You can paint any colour, with reduced preparation costs. 4. You can have durable metal without need to paint. 5. You reduce maintenance costs and repair costs.

Continued on next page

OFFER ANALYSIS SHEET
Product or Services: Prefabricated cubicles

FEATURES	BENEFITS	*which means that*	'YOU' APPEAL
All metal sections anodised.	1. Permanent protection. 2. Silver finish standard.		1. You have no maintenance costs. 2. You achieve good and attractive finish suitable for use with any colour chosen.
	3. Aluminium alloy.		3. You benefit in cheaper and quicker fixing and drilling on site, as some metal-working is allowed for in design to give adjustability on sizes.
	4. Wide range of sections and sizes readily available.		4. You have greater freedom in structural arrangements for special designs and requirements.
Wide variety of fixings and fittings available, plus accessories.	1. Adjustable pedestals if required.		1. You can accommodate floor-falls or unevenness without need of special packing-up.
	2. Nylon hinges and assembly cleats.		2. You avoid maintenance – non-rusting hinges require no lubrication. You simply achieve doors to self-close or open at minimum cost.
	3. Pilfer-proof screws, etc.		3. You reduce repair costs due to vandalism and pilferage.
	4. Special bolts, hinges, etc.		4. You can satisfy special requirements for invalid cubicles in the one package – thus your specifying time and costs are reduced.

12

Winning Commitment and Closing the Sale

Accuse any salesperson of working for a competitor and he will have good grounds to sue you for libel, yet many a seller does help his competitors to obtain orders. Although he sells so well that a buyer becomes very interested in the total proposition, he doesn't attempt to close the sale. The buyer is then able to consider alternatives – and one alternative could mean buying from a competitor.

At the end of a sales offer, a buyer can say 'Yes' or 'No'. It is then that so often she is allowed to get away with the delay excuse, 'I will certainly buy from you, but just leave it a few more days . . .'

Before the seller calls back, a competitor – perhaps a very strong closer – may see that buyer, with the advantage that the total proposition has already been sold for him. He need only concentrate on proving that his offer is tailored exactly to the buyer's needs to get the order.

There comes a time – perhaps on the first call, or even on the tenth call – when a buyer has complete understanding of the proposition – when she is obviously interested, and able to buy. It is then that a saeller must determine to obtain a decision.

Many salespeople, on losing an order, have said something like this:

> 'I'd have bet fifty to one I'd get that order. Everything was going fine – she even sent out for tea for us – then suddenly, at the very last minute, she changed her mind and told me she'd have to think it over. And I've learned what that means! In my part of the country if you don't get the order at the first real opportunity, you've generally lost it. I don't know what went wrong . . .'

Or another bewildered salesperson might say:

'I told everyone that the order for £50,000 was in the bag.
I've called on Lawrence regularly over the two months since
we received the inquiry – and, of course, I've known him for
years. We carried out a survey and he congratulated me on
the care taken. Also, I personally went to his factory to go
through his equipment point by point with everyone concerned. After I'd posted the quotation, I followed up with a
telephone call, and Lawrence told me that he'd never
received a clearer quote or one better laid out. He promised
to post us the order last Monday week, and l got all ready to
celebrate on the Tuesday. It didn't arrive. I telephoned on
Wednesday and he said he was getting it off for sure on
Thursday – but last Monday it hadn't turned up, and everyone at the office began ribbing me. I telephoned Lawrence
again this morning, and he told me the order had gone to
Whetherby's, our competitors. He explained that it wasn't
his fault – that the order had been all made out for us and
then his managing director, who apparently knows old man
Whetherby very well, insisted that they should get the
business. It's hardly credible, because they're five per cent
more expensive than we are. It makes you want to weep for
British industry, doesn't it?'

Promises, Promises

Probably because salespeople are usually optimists, they believe
time after time in promises made by industrial or retail buyers or
specifying authorities. It doesn't matter how often a seller learns
a bitter lesson – that buyers' promises can be broken – he still
says, 'This time I *know* we'll get the order.'

When selling consumer goods salespeople only meet closing
obstacles when they move away from order-taking and introduce
a new line, or try to increase the size of the order for a standard
line. As regular callers they will usually not get a direct rebuff, but
a promise to consider the matter later.

Too often, a sales agent misinterprets a delay-excuse for a
promise. Buyers use such phrases as:

'I'm sure it will be all right . . .'

'Don't worry – you know I'll do my best.'

'Leave it to me . . .'

'I'll have more shelf-space in a month or two.'

'If I have anything to do with it you'll get the business.'

These are not promises, yet on such airy phrases a seller will telephone his manager excitedly to tell him that the order has been won.

All sales staff know that an order is not definite until it has been sanctioned, but they still delude themselves into believing that the latest negotiation is different – a 'certainty' for them.

Orders are not generally lost on the seventh, eighth, or ninth call, when a buyer makes some weak reason for not being able to place the order. The order is usually lost on the very first call – or on the first call back after a quotation has been submitted – at the first attempt to sell a new line to a retailer.

At that first call, when the final decision is some way off, there is no need for a buyer to be too difficult, knowing that he will be seeing other salespeople and studying their propositions. But because at a first call a buyer is, apparently, receptive to a seller's offer, the salesperson sometimes forgets to sell – omitting to stress those extra benefits. Because that salesperson believes the order is a mere formality he doesn't resell when presenting the quotation, when there may still be doubts in the buyer's mind. Later, he wonders why he lost the order.

Sometimes quotations do not meet specifications. A supplying company may have a bad record for service, which weighs with a buyer; or they may employ a too-keen credit controller; or may not keep to delivery dates; or the value offered is not as good as that offered by a competitor. There are many reasons why orders are lost, but so often, they are lost through bad salespersonship.

There is an old selling tag: *A good sale closes itself*. While this is not strictly true, it does apply quite often, always provided the salesperson has not committed the selling sin of *stopping the buyer buying*.

There are four *stoppers* which make salespeople lose orders –

not at the last moment, but early in the sale. Here they are:

- talking on when the buyer is ready to buy
- not listening
- not giving proof
- not getting agreement, step-by-step

Talking on When the Buyer is Ready to Buy
When a seller doesn't ask for a decision but meanders on and on, repeating himself over and over again, a buyer loses concentration. His mind wanders, and during its wandering it can light on the fact that a competitor might be able to make a better offer.

Not Listening
Will Rogers once said: *If you listen more you may learn something.* This really does apply to salespeople.

Sometimes a buyer raises a query, or makes a comment, which the salesperson, being intent on selling, only half-hears. But if a seller doesn't give careful consideration to a buyer's viewpoint, he may brush aside the one factor which could make or mar a sale. The buyer's mind then switches off, and from then on he may nod his agreement, but he is thinking of other things. When the time comes to close the order, this agreeable buyer says, 'I'll think it over.'

If a seller is not certain whether he has heard correctly a buyer's remark, he should ask him to repeat it:

'Would you just explain that point again, Mr Brown?'

or,

'Have I got the point clear, Mrs Smith, is it . . .?'

Are you a good listener? Do you listen with your eyes as well as with your ears? Do you watch a buyer's face to see if it is indicative of his feelings? Does it mirror the strength of the point he is making? Do you look directly at him, so that he knows you are paying attention to what he is saying?

The hallmark of the bad listener is that he shows his lack of interest by looking in every direction instead of at the buyer.

Wandering eyes can mean nervousness, but more often than not this mannerism means lack of concentration. The non-listener not only misses vital points and brushes aside minor points, but he also annoys the buyer. So often a buyer has said (irrationally, of course), 'HE couldn't have sold to me if he'd given me a 30 per cent discount – I don't like his manner.'

So often the 'manner' means that the seller is taking too much and is not listening enough.

Try to think of someone you know who listens intently. Isn't he a likeable, popular person?

Now think of someone else who irritates and annoys you because he seems to want to monopolise all the conversation. He's disliked, isn't he?

Not listening is a closing stopper because:

1. The seller misses important points which indicate the buyer's real or lack of interest in the sales offer.
2. The buyer, in his turn, becomes a non-listener, which the seller believes indicates full acceptance of the offer. So when the buyer doesn't agree to purchase, the non-listener is baffled – he can't understand what went wrong at the last moment.

I hope he will now have that understanding.

Giving Proof
Buyers do not call salespeople liars, but does that imply that the buyer believes every word he is told? Of course not! It only means that most buyers are courteous, and see no sense in insulting a seller. But all buyers do, sometimes, have reservations and doubts about claims made by salespeople – that is why they ask questions. These questions may arise from doubts. The seller's answer can satisfy a buyer or leave him still perturbed. Even when a buyer apparently agrees with the answer he is given, he can still have reservations. That is why every salesperson should try to prove all major claims and as many minor claims as feasible.

A seller might say, 'It's actually 20 per cent faster,' or, 'Because of the linked switch it cannot cut out . . .' These are statements which a buyer may, or may not, believe. They should be proved by data explaining how the 20 per cent extra speed has been achieved and, perhaps, a technical report from an independent authority to confirm that the linked switch does stop cut-outs.

Another point to remember is that although benefits are derived from facts which, in turn, are given YOU appeal, the YOU appeal is not proof. For example, a seller might say:

> 'The whole unit is made of butalin, which is lighter than aluminium, so the unit can be fixed on a wall. This means that it will only occupy half the space of your present machine and will need only one operator instead of two. This saving in time and money . . .'

Here we have a fact, plus two benefits. But what proof is there that butalin is lighter than aluminium? And if it is, how much lighter – five per cent – 20 per cent – 50 per cent? Also, the buyer will want to have proof that only one operator is needed instead of two. Without adequate proof, the buyer may not argue the point, but he will mentally discount the claim.

It is important to prove as many points as you can. Do not leave that data brochure in your case because you have used it so often and now tend to neglect it. Pinpoint parts of a report which prove a particular claim. Whatever your company has given you in the way of proof, and whatever you have accumulated for yourself should be used at every call. Never believe that a buyer will necessarily remember, six months later, the proof shown to him earlier.

When a sale is in the final stages and is then, apparently, lost, the real reason could be not giving proof early, and then not reiterating that proof at a later call.

Not Getting Agreement Step-by-Step

For a seller to be reasonably certain that only a gentle nudge will be needed to get the order, he must progress the sale from the opening to its conclusion. This he achieves by constantly checking to make sure that the buyer understands, appreciates, and agrees with every feature, every benefit, every claim made – and is also satisfied with the proof given. This 'question and agreement' technique is known as *getting 'Yes' responses*. This is the form the question could take:

- 'Mr Johnson, you do agree, don't you, that the electronic shutter is right for your purpose?'
- 'It is essential for your purpose, isn't it, Ms Smith, that the area should be acoustically soundproof?'
- 'This advance in sophisticated micro-electronic technology can save you endless problems – you agree, don't you, Mr Brown?'
- 'You will admit that the automatic switch will save you money, won't you?'
- 'You prefer the better quality paper? Then . . .'
- 'You agree, Mr Williams, that it's a first-rate promotion?'
- 'It is a fast-moving line and that is what you want, isn't it, Mrs Lincoln?'
- 'The new carpet designs are attractive, aren't they, Mr Fellows?'

By getting a buyer's agreement all the way through the sale you are progressing towards an automatic close. There should be no attempt to close the order early in the sales offer because the buyer looks interested – no professional buyer will order until he had heard a complete proposition.

There are, of course, exceptions. For example, when a buyer needs and wants a product urgently, or when he has made up his mind to purchase in advance of the agent's call, or when a buyer knows that due to shortages he must stock up quickly, or wants to buy because the price is about to rise . . . the buyer will quickly show that he is in a buying mood. He is more friendly, will quickly ask questions about deliveries, discounts for quantities, etc., even take out an order book on the seller's arrival. In this buying situation, close as quickly as possible, to save your time and that of the buyer.

With these exceptions, a sale should only be closed on the completion of the offer, when the buyer, having heard all of the evidence, can make a decision. It is then that a buyer will often signal his intention to order, by asking pertinent questions.

These are the buying signals to look for at the end of the sales offer:

What she says:

- – 'Let me check the size again.'
- – 'I'm not sure about the finish – can you do it in . . .?'
- – 'Are you certain it won't . . .?'
- – 'What is the extra discount?'
- – 'I must be sure that your service engineers will give our customers quick service.'

What she does:

- • Studies the agreement and order form again
- • Picks up the brochure/catalogue/report/data sheet . . . and studies it very carefully
- • Operates the demonstration model once more
- • Picks up a sample and examines it closely
- • Looks towards the place suggested for the installation equipment
- • Looks again at the colour range
- • Calls in an assistant and talks approvingly about your offer

Ask:

You have completed your sales offer and believe that you have interpreted a buying signal correctly. What can happen?

1. The buyer says, 'Right, I'll have it!' or words to that effect.
2. The buyer still hesitates, waiting for you to prompt him for a decision. If you also hesitate, she will regain her authority and say, 'Call again towards the end of next week. By then I shall have a chance to . . . (speak to someone, see someone, think it over).'
3. You ask for the order.

The average seller so rarely asks for a decision. This is due to timidity or fear. The seller, afraid of receiving the reply 'No', would rather create a prospect than risk losing the order. He is quite happy to be told to come back next week – he is content; there has been no victory, but neither has there been a defeat.

This fear of asking for the order must be overcome if a seller is to succeed. Every buyer knows why salespeople are employed, and why they make calls – they want orders. Yet possibly as many as 30 per cent of all orders are lost because the seller will not ask the direct question, 'May I have the order?'

It need not always be as direct as this, but if it is, very few buyers will object.

The salesperson may prefer to say:

- 'You can always telephone me regarding after-sales service. Now let me note down the details.'
- 'I'll telephone the office straight away to have four units put aside for you.'
- 'I'm sure it will, Mr Smith, so shall we get the details settled?'
- 'You'll want it then, Mr Brown. If you will give me an order number now I can start getting the order processed.'
- 'I'll write the order up, Mrs Hope.'

If every seller made up his mind to ask for the order at every opportunity (that is, of course, whenever a buyer is able to give the decision) he would break every target set by his production manager.

CLOSING TECHNIQUES

There are many occasions when a hesitant buyer needs a 'nudge' before he will make up his mind, even after he has given buying signals. There are closing techniques which do enable a seller to urge the buyer gently towards making his decision.

The Alternative Close

If a prospective buyer is hesitant and doesn't give a clear buying signal, there is a risk in asking directly for the order. He could reply 'Yes', but he could also say, 'No'. If the answer is 'No', the seller is faced with the difficult task of persuading the buyer to change his mind.

By offering the buyer alternatives the seller is not inviting a 'Yes' or a 'No', he is only asking the buyer to tell him which of the alternatives he prefers. It is true he could answer, 'Neither', but remember, we are now dealing with the hesitant buyer, not with the one who has strong objections to buying. This buyer, who wants to buy but can't make up his mind, only requires very gentle persuasion to help him arrive at a final decision.

Here are examples of the *Alternative Close:*

- 'The unit can be installed in that corner or close to the sorting machine. Which do you prefer?'
- 'Would you prefer our cleaners to work early in the mornings, or after hours in the evenings?'
- 'Do you prefer the finish in grey, or black?'
- 'Do you want us to hold pending instructions, or deliver to site?'
- 'Do you want us to deliver the truck, or would you prefer to collect it from our depot?'
- 'Do you want a solid fixing, or would you rather the unit was easily moveable?'
- 'Do you require the extra-long extension, or would our standard 10 metre extension suit you?'
- 'Will you take 100 or 200?'
- 'Will you take advantage of our discount for 12 issues, or would you prefer to test the response by advertising in six issues to begin with?'

When the buyer states his preference, the seller should accept his answer as denoting a willingness to buy, and should begin to note down details or ask for the order number.

The Summary Close

Have you a good memory? If so, you are very fortunate. Many people can't remember what they said two minutes ago, let alone what someone else told them. The majority would be hard put to remember everything they were told during a recent conversation. That is why defence and prosecuting counsels and the judge summarise for the jury, to remind them of all the facts of the case.

At the end of the sales offer, the buyer may have forgotten a major benefit, so the seller must remind him of all the major benefits he has outlined during the sale.

For example:

> 'Mr Smith, all packages have advantages and disadvantages, but I believe that ours is the best, overall, for your application. It can handle up to six different currencies on both the bought ledger and the sales ledger, which is more than adequate for your division. It also enables you to generate five levels of costing details on each contract you run. You yourself said you cannot imagine you will ever need more than that. And it has complete open systems compatibility . . .'

> 'Mr Harris, I should like to sum up for you all the many advantages of Apex Automated Lathes. One, the Apex will handle parallel and taper turning, drilling and knurling. Two, it will handle your continuous operations, including, of course, internal and external threading. Three, a sophisticated programmer controls the hydraulically operated Apex. Four, a programme allows for six cross-slide and eight tail-stock operations. Five, your operator will be able to depend on a control panel which shows the cycle currently in operation.

> 'Mr Harris, I have stressed to you the benefits you will derive from each of these five features, but there is an additional one, which is that the Apex will cost you no more than any machine without these refinements. It only needs a power point, Mr Williams. Perhaps you would like to show me which one will be most convenient for you . . .'

The seller would not list every benefit – that would be too time-consuming, and because he has previously stated the benefits he can, as in the example of the Apex Automated Lathe, restate only the features and then turn then into a final benefit. On completion, the salesperson should always ask direct for the order, or offer alternatives.

The Caution Close
The caution close must be used sparingly. Many buyers react unfavourably to it. It can be effective for salespeople of goods or services in short supply, or insurance, fire-extinguishers, burglar alarms, or other safety devices:

- 'You will want me to give you cover right away, Mrs Johnson. After all, if someone dropped a lighted match in a waste-paper basket this afternoon and caused a fire, you would bear the loss. When I have your agreement to this policy, we bear the loss.'
- 'Mr Brown, as you know, the new Act could impose heavy fines if office conditions were unsatisfactory. You are too good a businessman to take the risk. I will see that you get delivery quickly.'
- 'With the season approaching, our delivery will extend to about six weeks. This won't be of any use to you. Be on the safe side, and place your order now, or competitors will carry stocks before you.'

Estate agents probably use this close more than others. They often have a waiting list for a house, and can honestly say, 'I am afraid you must make up your mind quickly, as there are two or three other people after it.'

Verbal-proof Story Close
Earlier in the sale you may have named your prospect other satisfied users of your equipment or service. But always try to save one verbal-proof story for the close. You might conclude like this:

- 'When I first called on Mr Smith of Smith & White, he was very dubious that our products would sell in his shop. His shop at Kenton is, as you know, very much like your own. He serves the same kind of people and stocks similar goods. I found it hard to convince him then that he would succeed with our merchandise. But he is a man of decision like you, and he placed a trial order. Now it is one of his best-selling lines – and it can be the same in your shop.'

Keep back a good story for the close – one that will swing the prospect in your favour.

The Isolation Close

One major reason usually prevents a prospect from buying. The salesperson must isolate it, in order to answer it. He asks the prospect for any such reasons, and writes them down.

'Let me be perfectly clear about what you want, Mr Brown,' he should say, and then begin to write:

'One, you don't like the standard of finish. Two, you cannot wait three months for delivery. Three, you want three months' credit from the date of installation. Is that so, Mr Brown?'

Mr Brown agrees, and then the seller takes each point and shows how it can be overcome. At last he isolates the main reason why the prospect does not sign the order. This may be lack of three months' credit terms.

'All that separates us, then, Mr Brown, is that you need extended credit facilities. Let me telephone our accounts department now and I can get it settled right away.'

'Influencing the Mind' Close

Salespeople of certain products cannot close an order. For instance, ethical pharmaceuticals are advertised only in medical journals and can be sold only through prescription. The doctor doesn't buy them and the chemist does so only when he gets a prescription for the drug. Although the seller cannot close the order, he must so influence the mind of the doctor that he will prescribe his drugs.

He again obtains 'Yes' responses, and may say at the end of the sales presentation:

'You will probably think it a good idea if I call on Smith's the chemists and tell them to be sure to have a stock available.'

or,

'You will find this drug so helpful that I am sure you will prescribe it over and over again, so I had better call at the chemist's and advise them.'

The sale cannot be closed, but the doctor's mind can be influenced; that, after all, is the same as a close.

Closing on a Minor Point

This is a form of trial close. The seller has lost little if the minor point is not acceptable to the buyer. He can continue with his sales offer and try to close again later.

Here are examples of *closing on a minor point:*

'You do prefer the anti-corrosive finish, don't you, Mrs Locke?'

'Would you like me to bring these drawings to you tomorrow morning?'

'Shall I arrange for an engineer to telephone you in the morning to talk about installation?'

'Don't you think it would be a change for the better, Mr Prior, if the print on the carton were changed from blue to red?'

'Do you like the idea of a pilot light being combined with a buzzer?'

'You'll need three showcards, won't you?'

'You will find our new display stand really does move the stock – you will, of course, want it . . .'

When the buyer agrees on the minor point, the seller again accepts that the order is his, notes down details, or offers alternatives.

The Concession Close

There are occasions when a seller is allowed to make a special concession to customers. This can be a standard quantity discount for orders of fifty units or more; as a special concession an agent might be allowed to offer this discount for only forty units. A guarantee could be extended from one year to two, as a boost for sales. Trading-in allowances could be increased; a survey for which a charge is usually made could be offered free; or there could be a special concession of a free supply for refills for machines. There could be a willingness to hold stocks to be drawn upon as required, or a guarantee to hold prices for six months; free delivery to site . . .

When a salesperson is allowed to make a special concession he usually uses it in his opening:

> 'Mr Jones, you will be pleased to hear that for orders of three hundred units placed now we will extend credit for six months without charging any interest . . .'

Why should that please Mr Jones when, possibly, he doesn't know at that stage whether he will need to place so large an order, or if he can use up the supply within the six-month period? If he can buy at a similar price elsewhere and pay monthly for the goods he may still be better off than placing an order for three hundred.

Until a buyer is persuaded that all the benefits offered, when added up, will make a purchase worth while for him, he may not be deeply interested in a special concession.

Even if a regular supplier offers a special concession, the buyer may try to get the concession without meeting the special demand of the supplier (taking immediate delivery, or a larger quantity, or stocking a new range of components . . .).

It is so much wiser, therefore, to hold back the concession and use it to help close the order. Then, when the buyer is mentally weighing up the pros and cons of the offer – when, perhaps benefits/costs stay equally poised – the salesperson may tip the scales in his favour by saying:

> 'Miss Smith, I am sure that the range of adhesives will be

of immense value to you, but as an extra incentive for you to buy now I can give you . . .'

'Our normal delivery is about eight weeks, sir, but I know you will benefit so much from the equipment when it is installed that I am going to put pressure on the works to make a concession in your case. I will see that you get delivery in three weeks. Is that all right, Mr Brown?'

'These showcards are very expensive and we are allowed to leave them only when we get orders in gross lots. Because I am sure you will succeed in selling the line I will make you a concession: you can have the showcard for a trial order of six dozen.'

'I am afraid that we don't, as a rule, supply fixing brackets. You can get these from your local DIY store. But as this is the first time we have done business together I will make a concession and arrange for you to have the brackets free.'

GET THE DECISION

You can use any combination of these closing techniques – you can summarise and then close on a minor point; or you can offer a concession and then close on an alternative; but if you use these closing techniques in a positive manner, if you will always ask for the order, you will undoubtedly close more orders and get more decisions.

After I had given a talk on salesmanship that stressed the need for a seller not to give in too quickly, the managing director of a company manufacturing cardboard containers came up to me. As he approached I recalled that he had once said: 'I hate the idea of salesmanship. My staff are representatives, not salespeople.'

Wryly I said to him. 'I understand you have no great faith in person-to-person selling.'

He smiled and answered, 'Oh, I've come a long way since I made that rather fatuous remark about salespeople. But I'm afraid I cannot agree with you about stickability. Why should someone be pestered by a salesperson when he has no intention of buying? If any salesperson tried that on me, I'd throw him out.'

The conversation went something like this:

A.T.   'Why do you employ salespeople?'

M.D.   'To show my goods and interest customers in them.'

A.T.   'Not to sell them?'

M.D.   'Of course they must also sell.'

A.T.   'And do they sell only to people who want to buy?'

M.D.   'Unfortunately not – that's why I have to employ them.'

A.T.   'Then you agree that to sell your goods the salespeople must influence the mind of the customer?'

M.D.   'Yes, I suppose so.'

A.T.   'Do you always buy because of a sudden impulse?'

M.D.   'No, of course not.'

A.T.   'You want the full facts.'

M.D.   'Yes.'

A.T.   'If you are given the full facts and you need a seller's product but still you decide not to buy, isn't it the duty of the seller to convince you that you are wrong?'

M.D.   'Yes, I suppose it is.'

A.T.   'What has happened is that either you are not clear about certain facts, or you want to examine competitors' prices before deciding.'

M.D.   'Well, that may be true.'

A.T.   'Do you want your salespeople to retire from a sale, so that your competitors can take over?'

M.D.   'Definitely not.'

A.T.   'That's what stickability means. If a seller has faith in his product he should exert himself to get an order at every opportunity. If he fails, the cause may be circumstances beyond his control – a bad presentation – or lack of stickability. You must agree with that.'

M.D.   'Well – yes, there is something in what you say. But I still don't like the sound of the word *stickability*.'

A.T.   'We needn't argue over words. You may prefer persistence or determination. But let me give you final proof: we carried out research amongst a panel of buyers, and learned from it that orders were frequently lost because the salesperson left while the buyer was still deliberating on the size of an order. Stickability only means staying a little longer. The stronger salesperson always does that – the weak one gives up too quickly.'

The managing director must have been convinced; he sends all his sales staff to us for training.

Stickability does not mean talking long after the full presentation has been given. It does not mean boring the prospect. It means probing, and asking questions to find why the buyer will not sign an order. Many buyers say 'No' for an answer.

The speciality salesperson knows that his best chance of completing a sale is at the first call; he can add nothing new to his presentation at subsequent visits.

Representatives selling consumer goods must also close sales at each visit (never become an order-taker). When lengthy negotiations must take place and quotations and drawings are submitted, no sale can be closed at a first call. The order, however, must be finalised as soon as there is a selling situation. It might be three months or a year after the first contact is made. But then, when the prospect has all the facts for a decision, the sale must be closed. This applies whether the order is for £100 or £100,000.

Many salespeople, asked to submit quotations, lose orders because they substitute the postal service for themselves. A postman can merely deliver a quotation; a salesperson can deliver, and sell. One of Britain's top sales agents selling engineering equipment takes every quotation to a prospect personally. He opens the interviews with:

'I have brought it to you personally so that we can go through it and make sure that we have met all your requirements.'

Then he sells all over again, and more often than not, he closes while his competitors are still writing letters and waiting for replies.

Remember – Polite Persistence Pays.

13

Answering Objections

Salespeople are sometimes given this advice:

> *Welcome objections, they prove that the buyer is interested and wants more information.*

Those who believe in welcoming objections obviously do not differentiate between *major* objections and *information-seeking* objections. Consider these remarks by buyers:

1. 'You tell me how we can use your tubing, when it is two inches wider in diameter than we need.'
2. 'But what about the fire risks with Telopolin? I read in the paper . . .'
3. 'I can't see much of a demand for them here.'

These are *information-seeking* objections and *are to be welcomed* because they do show that the buyer is interested.

The first buyer wants to know how he can dispense with manual labour and use, profitably, electronically driven units.

The second buyer wants to be told in which way he can benefit by using the larger diameter tubing.

The third buyer wants to hear that the risks of using Telopolin are minimal . . . And the fourth buyer wants reassuring that there will be a demand for the goods.

Yes, these buyers are definitely interested. But no seller should welcome *major* objections such as these:

1. 'Now you listen to me – I'll say it again: it is cheaper for us to use the manual labour of small manufacturers. I'm not switching to electronics in any circumstances.'
2. 'I have to work to specifications. Your inlet tube is two inches too large in diameter. Sorry, but it's no use to me.'
3. 'Telopolin? Do you realise the fire risk if I were to use it in our –? No thank you!'

4. 'There's definitely no demand for them here – I wouldn't stock them if you gave them away.'

Does any seller really welcome this type of objection? But whether he welcomes it or not, a seller has to close orders in spite of major objections or *information-seeking objections*, and here, he faces a problem – how to avoid antagonising a buyer.

Imagine this scene:

> While making final plans before leaving for a holiday a man says to his wife, 'We have to be at the airport an hour before take-off, so it's going to be a bit of a rush. We shall have to leave here at nine o'clock.'
>
> 'No we don't, dear,' answers the wife, 'we don't have to leave before half-past nine – we have to check in half an hour before take-off . . .'
>
> 'Look, I ought to know, I got the tickets, didn't I? The agent at Best's Travel told me –'
>
> 'Then you were told wrong – or you didn't hear what was said. I know it's half an hour, because Mary caught the same flight last week, and –'
>
> 'Oh – why do you always have to argue when I tell you I know? I was told –'
>
> 'But you don't know. You're making a mistake . . .'
>
> The husband is about to lose his temper when suddenly it comes back into his mind that the agent at Best's Travel had said 30 minutes, and not 60.

Now what does he do? Apologise immediately? Not likely! He either digs his heels in and insists that he is right, or walks out of the room muttering and then has to work out ways of getting to the airport one hour before departure, while ensuring that his wife doesn't make further inquiries and discover the truth.

None of us likes to be proven wrong, and this applies particularly to those with authority to buy; yet if a buyer raises an objection, a seller has to prove him wrong if there is to be any progress towards the close of the sale. And this must be achieved without an argument developing – without the buyer becoming annoyed, and without the seller creating the impression that he is more knowledgeable than the buyer.

The best technique for overcoming this problem is not to let the objection arise. Think again of the argument which developed between the man and his wife *after* he had told her that they had to be at the airport one hour before the flight.

If the wife had raised the issue herself, and had been able to prove conclusively that the time lag was half an hour, she would have forestalled her husband's categorical statement. No argument would have developed, because the husband would not have *voiced* his belief, and it is what is *said* that matters – not what is *thought*.

Nobody minds switching thoughts – most of us do it all the time. As others talk – explain – lecture, we often want to interrupt; but later when our doubts have been removed we are glad that we remained silent. Once we have spoken out we try to justify ourselves, right or wrong. When a buyer voices his objection, it becomes doubly hard to persuade him to alter his mind, and he will sometimes use ridiculous arguments, rather than admit he is wrong.

The objection of the seller when devising his sales offer is to forestall major objections, so avoiding a subsequent clash of ideas, with each buyer determined to prove his objection valid.

The first step in reaching this objective is to analyse objections; for only by a better understanding of the reasons for objections can a seller forestall them.

ANALYSING MAJOR OBJECTIONS

In the main, major objections fall into two groups: *primary*, and *selective*. When a buyer cannot see a need for a product, he raises a *primary* objection – he doesn't want to buy your product or service, or anyone else's.

For example, a managing director might decide that his company has no need for a knowledge management system. Time after time, he will refuse appointments to consultants, always using the *primary* objection, 'We have no need for a knowledge management system'.

When a buyer is in the market for a product service and has only to decide between competitive sales offers, he will raise with each competing salesperson *selective* objections relating only to a specific offer.

Primary Objections

It is a complete waste of time to stress general benefits in the face of a *primary* objection. Nearly always, when a *primary* objection is raised, there is an unrecognised need.

If a seller knows that a need exists, he must plan to sell the need (not the product) in his opening sentence, and forestall the *primary* objection. Let us consider, again, the example of the managing director who believes his company has no need for a knowledge management system.

The consultant who plans carefully uses these opening words:

'Mr Johnson, like you, many of my clients would not have given a moment's consideration to purchasing a knowledge management system even a year ago, but companies like AYZ have changed their views when they heard that data of all categories of projects run by all world-wide subsidiaries could be produced within one minute by using our software. And with all executives' time being so costly . . .'

Because that managing director suddenly realises the saving possible to him by having a quick response – and because he wants to know why the AYZ board changed its views when they heard of the new software – he will allow the seller to continue with the sales offer.

The success of this technique for dealing with a *primary* objection depends on the ability of the seller to work out an appropriate opening.

The Selective Objection

Objection analysis is necessary if a seller is to forestall major objections. The first step in this exercise is to consider objections raised by buyers, but because all buyers do not raise the same one, a complete list of all *selective* objections, major and minor, should be prepared. These will cover a wide field: price – design – size – weight – noise – durability – running costs – not up to a standard specification – not passed by an authority (fire department, insurance, etc.) – difficulty in fixing – supplier not carrying out own installation – satisfied with present supplier – storage problems – handling problems – employees against its use – past problems (customers let down over service, delivery, etc.) – no demand – over-stocked – not advertised enough – why should *A* be stocked when *B*, a similar product, sells so well?

The next step is to decide on the best answers to each objection listed.

Forestalling the Objection

The completed list of objections and answers should now be studied in conjunction with the sales offer analysis forms. Consider each feature/benefit to determine whether or not the YOU-appeal sentence should be altered to counter a possible objection.

For example, you are selling a piece of equipment which is noisy and an objection to the noise is raised at nearly every call. There is, however, a good reason for the noise. To quieten the unit would entail extra costs, and in the opinion of the marketing director the benefits you can offer far outweigh the noise factor. The noise is due to a mechanism which helps considerably to reduce the consumption of oil, while at the same time working at a faster rate and improving production. The design team felt there was no point in losing these advantages for the sake of quietness – but the objection arises time and time again, and is difficult to overcome in spite of the extra benefits offered.

In your sales offer you have already stressed the benefits of reduced oil consumption, etc., but the buyer, having perhaps been primed by a competitor, might say:

> 'That's all very well, but what about our operators who have to stand by the machine all day? The noise will drive them up the wall.'

What you have to do is to change slightly the YOU-appeal benefit sentence, before the objection arises.

You might say something like this:

> 'Mr Jones, the Star equipment, as you probably know, has been specially designed to give you reduced consumption of oil while, at the same time, stepping up production – and this is achieved without excessive noise. We haven't silenced the unit at your expense – as we could, so easily, have done; this would only have added to the cost for no real purpose . . .'

You will not, then, pause for comment by the buyer but continue to prove the savings, and later seek a 'Yes' response. Having put the issue in its true perspective, the molehill of noise has not become a mountain – a crescendo of sound – in the buyer's mind. When you re-emphasise the saving in cost due to the rational thinking of your design or Research and Development department, you take the sting out of a competitor's claim, while discounting the noise factor. If it were not for the competitor's claims, the buyer would perhaps not have raised the objection at all.

Although the buyer may have the noise factor in mind when the seller begins his sales offer, this can change while the saleeller is stressing the advantages of the unit. If the objection has been successfully forestalled, the buyer may think along these lines:

> *We're always getting complaints about noise and draughts – or it's too hot, or too cold . . . It's probably no noisier than the hydraulics in B shop . . .*

It is worth remembering that nearly everyone exaggerates when attempting to prove a point – and buyers, especially, are prone to exaggeration. Why a buyer tells you the price is 20 per cent too high, he usually means about five per cent. When he tells you he can get delivery from X by return, he probably means in two weeks, but he will buy from you if you can do better.

To get a realistic figure, you should always, mentally, tone down a buyer's claim.

Imagine now that you are selling vending machines to be installed on the factory floor, available for use at any time of the day. You will often meet the standard objection:

> 'That's not for us! Why, they'd be crowding round the machine all day – the loss of time would be much too high.'

You forestall this objection by saying:

> 'Mrs Williams, the great advantage of installing these machines on the factory floor is that you will maintain production. As you know, Mrs Williams, during the day there are always fatigue times when, however conscientious employees may be, they begin to feel weary and ease off. When they are allowed to have a quick cup of tea or coffee, you will find the fatigue time to be counteracted. But I know exactly how you feel, Mrs Williams. You can imagine a day-long queue by the machine – and this will happen to a small extent for the first day or so. After that, facts prove that there is no more time taken up when the machines are in use than in normal break-periods. That is why they have been installed by X, Y, and Z. Think of the benefit to you of having these machines on the shop floor – better morale, no falling off of output during peak fatigue hours . . .'

If you are selling tubing, you might be met regularly with the objection:

> 'I can get exactly the same from X, there is no need for me to open a new account.'

Once more, you may want to forestall the objection. You can say:

> 'Mr King, I am not claiming that our tubing is less expensive or more expensive than any other. But I can claim that with us you are assured of outstanding service, which has to be experienced to be appreciated. We . . .'

By emphasising early in the sales offer the outstanding service your company gives, you may remind a buyer that the standards of his present suppliers are not as good as they may have been in the past.

Many sales agents regularly meet the objection:

> 'I want immediate delivery – I can get them quicker elsewhere.'

If you know you cannot deliver your products quickly, it would be wrong to make any rash promises. You can forestall the objection in this way:

> 'I know, Mr Thomas, that you will want deliveries as quickly as possible – but I also know that nothing would get past you if it were not manufactured to the highest standards. Our quality product has to pass through six separate tests. When we deliver in nine weeks' time, you will not need to put them through any tests yourself – they are guaranteed by us . . .'

Now imagine that you are in a shop, wanting to buy a shirt. You ask for one in pale grey. The assistant hasn't one in stock, but shows you a shirt in pale grey with a dark grey stripe.

> 'Do you like this?' he asks.
>
> 'No,' you reply, 'I don't think stripes are fashionable any more.'
>
> The sales assistant quickly says, 'Well, we sell a lot of them.'
>
> 'Possibly you do,' you answer rather coldly, 'but I don't think they are fashionable.'

The assistant can argue; he won't win. He has implied that you are not fashion-conscious – that you are not aware that striped shirts are again being worn. The more he argues, the more loyal you will be to the anti-stripe brigade. You may even like stripes, but you wouldn't admit this to the assistant. For you, it is now a plain shirt, or nothing.

Most of us would respond similarly to the assistant's clumsy answer to the objection, 'I don't like striped shirts.' But the scene could be played differently. The assistant hasn't a plain grey shirt in stock, but the nearest to it is a plain grey with a stripe. He guesses you may object to the pattern, so he forestalls you by saying:

> 'As you know, stripes have come right back into fashion again. Here is the very latest in grey, with a darker grey stripe. I thought you would like to see it – it does something for the shirt, don't you think, sir?'

'Sir' will probably buy.

Here are some instances of forestalling objections:

1. A seller is demonstrating a car. He knows that it is rather sluggish when pulling away from a standing start, so he says:

> 'We have purposely avoided a jerky or racy getaway from a standing start. Most people know the dangers of trying to get ahead of other motorists when the traffic lights change to green. But the main reason this car is made to glide away instead of jumping off is to save petrol. It helps you to get at least 60 miles to the gallon. That appeals to you, Mr Brown, doesn't it?'

The objection, 'Why doesn't the car get away faster?' has been forestalled.

2. A fire extinguisher salesperson knows that it is a large object, and prospects may complain of its size. He says:

> 'Miss Jones, one of the advantages of our extinguisher is its size. Because it is fairly large and robustly built, it holds 50 per cent more water than the average extinguisher – just the extra you may need to kill a fire completely. And it can be easily seen – everyone knows where it is. So many smaller types are put away in a drawer, and no one can find one when it is wanted. You like this design, don't you?'

The objection, 'It seems too large for a private house,' has been forestalled.

You will never attempt to forestall every objection; you should only try to forestall those objections which either you meet time and time again, or you know will be raised by the buyer you are calling upon.

Your objective is *not* to put controversial issues in the buyer's mind, but to forestall major objections.

The Brush-off Objection

Here are examples:

> 'I'm sorry but Mr James is suddenly very busy and can't see anyone else today.'
> 'I'm not interested, thank you.'
> 'I'm far too busy to discuss this matter now.'

This form of objection can be met even if the interview is by appointment. Here are the standard answers:

> 'I'm so sorry I caught him at the wrong moment, but . . .'
> 'It is because you are so busy that you will be interested to hear about . . .'
> 'It's my fault, Mr Smith. Obviously, I haven't made it clear . . .'

Unfortunately, these answers rarely work – although they should always be tried. When a seller meets a quick brush-off it is sometimes better for him to leave, research to discover what the buyer really needs, and return with an opening more suitable to those needs. On a subsequent visit he may find the buyer in an entirely different mood.

There is often a reason for the quick brush-off – especially if an appointment has been made. Assuming that the seller has not annoyed the buyer in any way by his manner, bearing, the words he uses or the clothes he wears, it may be that the buyer has just had 'one of those days' – problems with the staff, problems with the managing director . . . he may have been reprimanded, his budget may have been cut, perhaps he has had a quarrel at home before leaving for the office . . .

It is almost an adverse selling situation, but not quite. If the seller is always aware that a brush-off is possible he can plan to meet it by having ready in his mind a special benefit to suit that particular buyer. He can say:

'Of course I won't worry you this morning, but may I leave you with one thought: our Nufix will take away all risk of an electrical breakdown.'

One key sentence such as this can change a brush-off into an invitation to stay. Although the buyer may be in a black mood, or his mind is on other matters, he is still a buyer, and if he has experienced problems which the salesperson suggests can be overcome, the buyer may quickly change his mind and want to hear more.

The Delay Objection

Even efficient buyers who place orders every day do not always come to quick decisions. Regular buyers in factories, offices and shops can be equally slow. Retailers place orders for consumer goods and would not delay signing an order for their routine requirements. If, however, they are asked to buy new products or capital equipment for their shops, they often postpone a decision.

Many of us are undecided when we are in a position to buy. Even buying shoes, we often cannot make up our minds. When negotiating for a house, it is difficult to decide whether A or B is better. We are all tarred with the same brush, and we all invent delay excuses. If we look at an item of furniture in a shop we may tell the assistant that we want to check our own furnishings before a decision. When an insurance salesperson calls we try to put him off until we have more time – perhaps after our holiday. This, of course is sheer nonsense. If it is right to take out additional insurance, then the quicker the better. Nothing is gained by delaying matters for a few weeks. If we are presented with a detailed proposition by a seller, we should be able to make up our mind on the spot. There is nothing new to be learned at a later interview. But we will still try to delay matters.

When a delay excuse is used, a prospect is only partly sold. His interest has been aroused but not his enthusiasm. If he suggests you should call back at a later date he will think of all the reasons *not* to buy before you come again. he will not think of a single reason for placing an order. He may also buy from a competitor before you return.

The seller must counter these excuses by trying to find the real reason for the delay:

> 'I appreciate, Miss Brown, that you would like to leave matters for two or three weeks, but maybe I haven't explained everything fully to you. Again, let me go through all the reasons why this policy can be of value to you, and perhaps you will tell me if there is any point you are not clear about.'

> 'I can understand that you want to consult your partner, but is that fair to him? He won't have the complete proposition before him as I have tried to put it to you, so he may veto the whole idea, and this could cause a loss for both of you.'

> 'Mr Jackson, I do understand that you would like to see me again in about three weeks. Before I started this job I had six months of intensive training, and I have now been with the company for five years. All this has helped me to give a better service to our customers. It also means that I have been trained to explain to you fully every facet of our service. If you wish to put our proposition to your Board of Directors, you will agree, Mr Jackson, that it would be almost impossible to be fair to everyone. No doubt you would prefer me to address your Board. But don't you think they would prefer you to come to a decision that will benefit the whole business?'

> 'Mrs Smith, you are in business to make profits, isn't that right? Now, when this equipment is installed you will make extra profits right away. Let's take a small amount of £200 profit in six months. (This may be from extra turnover, reduced absenteeism, or labour costs, etc.) It would mean that our equipment, which now costs £1,000, will cost you, in effect, £3,000 in six months, because we must then include the £2,000 you have lost. Don't you think it is right for you to decide now?'

> 'Mr Brown, you have built up your business by making

decisions – decisions based on facts. I have given you the facts and so I am sure you will, like Mr Whiting of Smith & Co., want to place your order right away. As I told you, he has been delighted with his purchase – and so will you be.'

Making the Decision

The delay objection is not, on the face of it, an objection against buying, but against arriving at an immediate decision.

Here are examples:

- 'I want to think again about the fixing problem – come and see me next week.'
- 'I'll have to see my partner (co-director – manager) as she is involved in the design of this job (or in buying canned merchandise – purchasing electrical goods, etc.).
- 'It's a bit over the price limit – I'll have to put it before the Board.'
- 'Although your offer seems right there are other factors that have to be considered.'
- 'As it might mean a change in our production line I shall have to speak to R and D first.'
- 'As it is partly to do with transport I shall have to discuss it with Mr Neville.'

When, just before the moment of decision, a buyer says, 'I must see Neville about this,' it is nearly always an excuse to delay the decision. Otherwise, very early in the sale (and this applies especially if the negotiations have taken place over a long period) the buyer will tell the salesperson that Mr Neville will have to be involved. In fact, a buyer, if interested in a proposition, will gladly arrange a meeting between the seller and anyone else who may be involved in the buying decision.

For all that, a seller cannot accept a delay excuse and walk out. He must try for the full support of the buyer if Mr Neville is to be convinced.

He should say something like this:

'I appreciate that Mr Neville must be consulted, but if, at this moment, the decision were solely yours, would you place the order?'

If the buyer is hesitant, or gives a negative reply, the seller will know that he has not proved his case. He will then have to discover the real reason why the buyer will not arrive at an immediate decision. Generally, however, the buyer using a delay objection is using the excuse to avoid making a decision. He is not sure – he wants to think it over . . .

But what is there for him to think over, if he has been given a complete sales offer in an hour – a day – a week – or over a period of weeks or months? The thinking time is when he is with the salesperson. That is when he can ask questions, and clear his mind of doubts. We know, therefore, that most delay objections are not valid. The problem facing the seller is to discover a buyer's real reason for delaying his decision.

All delay objections, if genuine, are raised early in the sale. When discussing design, a buyer will tell the salesperson that this is a subject that he will have to discuss with the R and D Department, his project engineer, or his chief buyer. A change in the production line will, obviously, involve others. But if these delay reasons (not objections) are *not* made clear early in the sale the buyer usually doesn't have to delay buying. If he is apparently satisfied on all points of the sales offer but still says, 'Leave me a leaflet (catalogue, drawing, etc.)' then he is, most certainly, not satisfied with one or more of the features of the product or service.

There is always a reason for the delay-excuse, and the reason is usually one that the buyer doesn't want to disclose to the salesperson. It is a

hidden objection.

Yes, buyers do hide their true objections from sales agents, time and time again. That is why they occasionally seem to act irrationally.

What perturbs a salesperson is that, in spite of a good presentation and getting 'Yes' responses, a buyer will say, 'No, leave it for a week or so.' At such a moment, many salespeople do not know what action to take. They have answered every objection the buyer has raised – except one: the buyer is hiding from them.

It is said of Talleyrand, the French diplomat well versed in the double-talk of politicians, that when he was told that a foreign envoy would not be arriving at a conference for the very good reason that he had died on the way there, Talleyrand answered, 'Yes, but I wonder what the real reason was for his not coming.'

Let us first consider what a salesperson can do to find the real reason for the delay objection. He can say,

> 'I appreciate, Ms Johnson, that you would like to leave the matter for two or three weeks, but what is there to think over? Perhaps I haven't explained everything clearly.'

To which he will nearly always receive the reply, 'No, you have done very well. Everything is very clear. Just leave it for now.'

When a seller knows early in the sales offer that someone else is involved in the buying decision, he will, of course, ask to be allowed to see that person (or committee or Board). But when he is not sure of the validity of the objection, he might say:

> *'Mr Jackson, forgive me if I take up another ten seconds of your time by blowing my own trumpet. I have been with my company some time as you know, and I have not only had six months of intensive training, but have attended refresher courses every year. This enables me to give a better service to our customers, and also to explain fully every facet of our product. Do you think that perhaps I should come and talk to . . .'*

The answer will, invariably, be, 'You can leave it to me. I have all the facts at my finger-tips, and I promise I'll do the best I can for you.'

He won't, because he is not sure himself whether or not he should buy. He has an objection unanswered, because he has hidden it from the salesperson.

The effective technique you can use to find the hidden objection is to invite the buyer to finish a sentence – a sentence, which, instinctively, he will assume is based on knowledge.

When a buyer is unexpectedly asked to voice a thought in this way you will hear the truth, more often than not.

The technique is also based on a key phrase:

'And may I ask your *other* reason for not deciding now?'

Look straight at the buyer while you are speaking and begin the sentence on a low note, finishing with a slightly higher inflection.

This technique must not be used at any time other than at the close. It would be quite wrong to seek the hidden objection earlier in the sale, when the buyer has not heard the complete sales offer. Also, the exact words must be used; to change them to, 'Is there any other reason for your delaying buying?' would, inevitably, bring a negative reply. The direct question which invites a 'Yes' or a 'No' will usually get a 'No'.

If a salesperson is continually meeting a delay objection it is because:

1. The sales offer is incomplete.
2. The salesperson does not ask for the order. When the time arrives he is too timid to request a decision, leaving it to the buyer to say something. And the buyer usually raises a delay objection.
3. The seller has not built confidence. Then the buyer, in his turn, becomes timid, is fearful of making a mistake, and so delays matters.
4. There is a hidden objection, which he has not been able to answer.

The Price Objection
There is no magic answer to the buyer who says, 'You are too expensive, I can buy cheaper.'

There are, of course, selling platitudes which are to be used regularly by salespeople, but nowadays they usually antagonise buyers – for example:

– 'Do you always buy the cheapest, Mr Jones – the

cheapest suit, the cheapest car . . .?'
- 'Nothing is so expensive as something that is cheap.'
- 'There is nothing manufactured that someone else cannot produce cheaper.'
- 'You get what you pay for.'

Although these often repeated sentences rarely help, well-thought-out answers are essential in helping to overcome a price objection. But first you should study the reasons why buyers react unfavourably to price and, equally important, you must analyse your own thinking on the whole subject.

The Price Objection

Under normal circumstances, most salespeople face price objections continually, not necessarily because a buyer believes he can buy more cheaply, but because he wants to obtain a discount, if possible. Unfortunately, however, too many salespeople believe that they are singled out and their products condemned because of the pricing policies of their companies.

Is there a production manager anywhere in the world who has not been told by a seller that he is being priced out of the market? (Our training organisation has associate companies in forty countries and the price objection is always of the most concern to *all* sales agents.) Sometimes a salesperson's fear of price is quite irrational, but while positive thinking won't help him much – *my price is not too high, my price is not too high, my price is not too high* – negative thinking – *my price is too high, everyone knows my price is too high* – is disastrous.

First then, every seller should decide how to defeat his own fear of the price objection. He should begin by asking himself two questions:

1. Would my company still be in existence if our products were so over-priced?
2. As I have been taking orders at our standard prices, why should those buyers be so incompetent as to buy from me if they could buy better elsewhere?

The next step in defeating the price bogey is for a seller to meet an agent employed by one of his competitors. This is not difficult, because salespeople meet each other all the time – on trains, in waiting rooms, in car parks . . .

He should ask the other salesperson this question:

'Why do you always undercut your prices?'

Back will come the reply, instantly:

'Well, I like that! My company undercut prices? That really is the pot calling the kettle black. It's your people who keep reducing the prices.'

If only salespeople could attend sales conferences of other companies in any field of activity they would find that at question time someone always raises, and condemns, the pricing policy.

Sales staff are rarely singled out for the price objection. It happens to everyone, but while some agents wait, almost expectantly, for the *blow* of a price objection, the successful seller is quite proud that he does not compete on price, but competes very strongly on value.

He will say to a buyer, 'Not only do we give you all these benefits, but in addition we guarantee a twenty-four-hour service. And the price is *only* . . .' because he believes that the price is relatively low compared with the value he is offering.

Remember, it is always value which determines the price the buyer will pay.

The Buyer's Attitude to Price

It is a buyer's function to spend his company's money to the best advantage. His first consideration is to fill the exact need at the lowest possible price.

To achieve his aim his thoughts may conflict with the objections he voices. For example:

A buyer says: 'You are 20 per cent too dear.'
He thinks: *It's about five per cent more than Brown's offer, but it will have a longer life, and that saves constant changes. I'll try to get him down in price – if not, I'll buy anyway.*

A buyer says: 'You are much too expensive for our needs.'

He thinks: *I have had so much trouble with Smith's, perhaps I should change over – pay a little more and get something more reliable . . . and save myself some headaches, as well.*

A buyer says: 'I can show you competitive quotes and you'll see that you're way out.'

He thinks: *These people do give world-wide service, and that's what our export people have been asking for, for a long time.*

If the minds of these buyers could be read, the salespeople could so easily close the sales by:

1. re-stressing the value of the long life of the product.
2. stressing the quality of the product.
3. stressing the value of world-wide service

It is said that a dog can tell instinctively if a human being is afraid. Buyers certainly have a sense which tells them whether or not they can take advantage of a seller's fear of price.

Buyers have told us over and over again that although they always feel it is part of their job to raise the price objection, they are also sending out a challenge: *Convince me that it is in my interests to pay your price.*

When to Introduce the Price

It is possible on many occasions to forestall a price objection if a seller is able to heap benefit on benefit before he gives the price. Although that should be the seller's aim, whenever he is asked the price by the buyer, he must not stall. Hesitation could be taken as a reluctance to give the price because it is too high.

The only exception to this rule is if the price cannot be given until a survey has been made – additional information obtained – or it is necessary to have a better understanding of a buyer's exact needs. Only then may the seller answer: 'I can't tell you exactly now, because . . .', or, 'The price would depend on . . .'

His objective, however, must be to give as many benefits as possible *before* introducing, or being asked, the price.

Answering the Price Objection

Whether the price objection is used by a buyer to attempt to obtain an extra concession, or in the genuine belief that he could buy better, handling the objection is the same; the sellermust concentrate the mind of the buyer on price difference.

For example, a seller quoting ten units at a total price of £1,200 may be told by the buyer that he could purchase similar units for £1,000. The salesperson says:

> 'Mr Jones, it is true our price is £120 a unit, and the price you want to pay is £110 a unit; but Mr Jones, think what you will get for that extra £10.00 – and *it is only* £10.00 a unit. Firstly, we guarantee . . .'

The seller would then stress the advantage of his product over any similar product the buyer could purchase.

Always pinpoint the *difference* in price – is it 5 per cent or 10 per cent, is it £10 or £20, or £200 or £20,000? Nearly every buyer will give some indication of the price he will pay unless, of course, he is considering tenders. Assuming the difference arrived at is £500 of the total quotation, the seller must set out to prove the extra value the buyer would receive for *only* £500.

What Does it Cost?

One of our greatest trainers, and my most experienced colleague, had his own personal solution to the price objective. He said:

> 'In almost every sales situation the price must be justified. This is, of course, always true when it is overtly raised. 'It's too expensive' is a typical comment, and it can't pass unchallenged. Every sale is an investigation, and it is vital to pinpoint the reasons underlying a buyer's opinion. For example, it is always reasonable to query the word "expensive". What does it mean? Expense is not an absolute, and makes sense only in relation to another figure.'

Here is an example:

> 'Mr Buyer, you say it is too expensive, and I understand

why. I agree with you that it is not cheap, but when you say "expensive", please tell me – in comparison with what?'

This question begins the process of investigation, and his answer indicates the buyer's reasoning. The answer may be anticipated, for choices are limited.

If your product/service is not being used, these are the choices:

- To use a similar product
- To have a similar service
- To use a similar method
- To use similar raw materials
- To do without altogether.

The answer gives a basis for discussion. Through product knowledge, an awareness of the customer's needs and of the performance of competitive products, an objective comparison can be made. The process of cost justification can begin.

Price is an important factor in a sales negotiation, but it does not always dominate the situation. People do not buy on price alone. Sometimes the seller is more conscious of price than the buyer! The mere use of the word contributes to the problem. It is an outgoing word, suggesting spending. Sales staff should cultivate the use of the words 'cost' and 'investment'. These are commercial expressions that sound more professional.

In discussion, and particularly in answer to the question, 'How much is it?' the seller should use, 'It costs only . . .' This clearly and simply indicates the salesperson's confidence in the offer he is making, as does, 'Your investment will be only . . .'

The price objection, like any other, must be answered in terms of benefits. The cost of the product/service, irrespective of the amount, must be shown as a valuable investment for the purchaser. The analysis of value is cost justification. Value has three distinct and important elements, and each must be explained and illustrated to the buyer in terms of benefits:

Efficiency
Every product or service has a demonstrable and measurable

rating of performance. This is its efficiency.

Economy

Every buyer looks for economy, and the features of a product or service that provide it must be fully described. Economies, not technicalities, are the reasons for buying.

Faster production, savings of time and labour, more miles per gallon, longer life in use – these are a few examples.

Profit

To the buyer concerned with the distribution and resale of a product – a wholesaler or a retailer – one important aspect of value is profit. The product must be efficient and economical in performance, but it must be shown to be profitable. A first glance at the proposed percentage mark-up may suggest that the product will be less profitable than existing stock items, or others on offer. There may be instances of this, but it is important to investigate and establish the true facts. For example, product A is bought at nine units and sells at 12, but product B costs eight and sells at 12. The obvious reaction is that product B is more profitable. But profit on one item of sale is not the only consideration. Other factors must be rated:

- What will be the repeat-business level?
- Is the quality right?
- Is the pack attractive?

Most important, what advertising, merchandising, or other promotional activity is part of the offer? This support for the distributor's sales effort is valuable. All aspects of this must be stressed to a buyer as an aid to his decision.

Service

A constant factor of any offer is service. The support of the distributor is a specialised form of service, but it exists in many other forms.

The advice of a technical representative is service.

The activity of the manufacturers' design staff on behalf of a potential customer is service.

The training of the customer's staff in the correct operation of newly installed equipment is service.

Not only are they service, but they are benefits, and should be sold as part of the total value of the offer.

Each element of value must be fully explained, and the buyer must understand how it will benefit him. Not only must he understand, but he must accept that the additional cost is justified in terms of value.

THE LOYALTY OBJECTION

This objection will be met by nearly all salespeople selling repeat products (component parts, chemicals, oils, packaging materials, accessories, consumer goods, etc.). It is usually only encountered at a first call and is possibly the most difficult of all objections to overcome.

Here are buyers' reasons for their reluctance to change suppliers:

1. 'We have been with Smith & Co for thirty years. I've been dealing with them myself for fifteen years, and before that our managing director, who in those days did his own buying, formed a friendly relationship with Tom Smith. They have always given us good service, so there is no point in my changing suppliers at the moment. Of course, if ever things altered . . .'

2. 'We are one of Brown & Co's largest customers, and no doubt because of this they look after us very well. We have only to telephone and they do everything to give us express delivery, or accept the return of unsuitable goods. If every they should let me down I shall be prepared to consider . . .'

3. 'It's a case of we buy from them – they buy from us. That's fair enough, isn't it? I can see no point in changing . . .'

These objections stem not so much from loyalty – although this does play a part – but from confidence in a supplier who has given good service for a number of years. Why should a buyer change when, over a period of time, he has had no real cause for complaint? A buyer will only make an immediate change if another supplier can offer similar value plus extra benefits – better price, better delivery, better design, something new, etc. With repeat products, a sudden great advantage of one supplier over another is rare, but no seller can admit defeat when meeting this very difficult objection and there are practical actions that he can take.

First, he must remember the selling axiom:

When all things are equal a buyer buys from the seller he likes the best.

This axiom should remind him to check up on himself, not because his aim is to ingratiate himself with a buyer, but to make sure that he does not annoy the buyer in any way – that could be a mistake made by the opposition, especially if their sales agent on the account changes.

In any event, over a number of years the regular suppliers are apt to take a buyer for granted, while if they employ a newcomer to the territory he may not know – or may forget – that his objective at each call is to sell; he may become lackadaisical or off-hand, and antagonise not only the buyer, but also other members of the staff.

A seller's efforts to please a buyer may not result in an order on the first call, third call, fifth or sixth call, possibly, but eventually the buyer's mind can be influenced by the seller's friendly personality – by his enthusiasm – and because he is so obviously keen to obtain the business.

If salespeople could hear buyers talking to their staff, they might well hear something like this:

'I always like that fellow – he's keen, persevering, and always well-mannered. We'll give him a break one day.'

Here are other positive steps the salesperson can take:

1. He must have an objective at each visit and never make the call hoping that something will turn up. The '*Anything for me today?*' type of approach is very unprofessional.
2. Even at the risk of being boring, at each call he should say to

the buyer something like this:

> 'I really do appreciate the reason for your loyalty to Smith
> & Co, but as I have told you before, Mrs Jones, it is my
> ambition for us to have the same opportunity as Smith's had
> so many years ago – the opportunity to prove to you that we
> can offer a similar – naturally, I feel sure that we can offer a
> better – service.'

or,

> 'Mr Harvey, it is impossible to read the future, but
> imagine that a problem occurs – perhaps a part of Smith's
> factory burns down – fires happen more frequently in Asia
> than in Europe – or there could be a transport delay from
> the Far East . . .Wouldn't you like to know that in such an
> event you had another trusted supplier to help you over a
> difficult period? Naturally, when things were right again you
> would want to return to Smith's and that, I think, is only fair.
> We are only aiming for a part of your business. If you will
> only test us now under normal conditions, you will prove for
> yourself that . . .'

To obtain a share of worthwhile business from a buyer who
refuses to open a new account a seller must have patience and
perseverance, sell on each call, and sooner or later he will get that
business.

Why? Because the majority of salespeople calling on that
supplier give up too readily, or make a series of 'Anything for me
today?' calls.

TECHNIQUES FOR HANDLING OBJECTIONS

1. *Don't interrupt – listen.* All too often, salespeople do not allow the
buyer to complete his objections. Because a seller is so sure that
he knows what the buyer is thinking, and believes he has the
answer, he interrupts, and, by doing so, never hears the complete
objection.

For example, the buyer may say, 'Yes, that's all very well, but the lining . . .'

The seller, feeling sure that the buyer is concerned about the strength of the synthetic fibres used in the lining, interrupts with:

> 'Please don't worry about the lining, Mr Green. We can strengthen it by using an interlining as well.'

The seller may have put into the mind of the buyer a query about the quality of the lining, when perhaps the buyer only wanted to criticise the texture, colour, finish . . .

The buyer should always be allowed to give his objection in full. He must not be interrupted and, equally important, the seller must look as though he is interested. His demeanour must not suggest that he has heard it all before and is eager to give the answer.

No one likes a *too clever* person, and when sales staff interrupt with pat answers, they may appear *too clever*, and may lose that buyer's confidence.

Always listen carefully to the buyer's complete objection, and then he will listen to your answer.

2. When an objection has been dealt with, do not return to it later in the sales offer.

3. For a salesperson to be certain that he fully understands an objection, it is sometimes wise to repeat it.

4. *The Empathy Technique.* We know that a relaxed buyer decides more readily. We know that tensions build up in a buyer just before he comes to a decision, and often prior to his raising an objection. He makes his point, and waits for the reaction. But no seller wants a battle, and if he is unable to forestall the objection, he must try to remove the tension from the buyer. By using the *empathy* technique, he indicates that he understands the objection, and the buyer, thinking he has won his point, relaxes.

Remember that the seller only empathises and understands: If the buyer raises an objection that the price is too high and the seller answers, 'Yes, it is high, but . . .' the buyer may relax, but the seller will find it very hard to convince him that the price is right, having once agreed with the buyer. The emphasis is on *understanding* – for example, one could say:

> 'I can understand your thinking at this stage that the extra investment may not be worth while, but . . .'

The salesperson is only showing the buyer that he understand his way of thinking, but he is not agreeing with him.

> 'On the face of it, Mr Smith, it does seem right that extra labour might be needed. However . . .'
>
> 'Your concern about the viscosity of the oil, Mr Johnson, is understandable, but . . .'
>
> 'I quite see your point of view, Ms Green, I'm glad you raised it. On the other hand . . .'

Remember, the *empathy* technique relaxes the buyer, slows down the pace of the sale, does not make a seller appear too clever and shows courtesy, because the sales agent shows that he appreciates the buyer's point of view.

The All-important Technique
A seller may know the answer to every objection that could be raised, but if he pounces – appears glib – argues – and doesn't use the *empathy* technique, his knowledge will be of little use to him.

To succeed in selling, the techniques for answering objections are just as important as the possession of a storehouse of answers to every objection.

14

Buyers' Views on Salespeople

What really matters to our customers and prospects? We may think we know, but do we really? Wouldn't it be useful to see ourselves through other eyes – the eyes of our (*potential*) buyers?

TACK's latest research on what buyers value in sellers gives us some valuable feedback.

What Buyers Don't Like

In order of priority:

1. An unacceptable manner	: insincere; arrogant; interrupting; disrespectful.
2. Poor presentation	: ill-prepared; too superficial; poor use of visuals or support materials.
3. Lack of knowledge or information	: ignorance about buyer's company; lack of product knowledge; lack of knowledge about seller's own company/ prices/terms, etc.
4. Time wasting	: lateness; irrelevant talk; talking too much or too long.
5. Insensitivity	: not discovering buyer's needs; aggression; pressure or 'pushiness' of any kind.

What Buyers Value Most

In order of priority:

1. A positive manner	:	polite; pleasant; sincere; alert; honest.
2. Good knowledge	:	of buyer's company; product and market knowledge.
3. Good presentation	:	clear; concise; well-prepared.
4. Sensitivity	:	good listener; discerns real needs; doesn't try to sell where no need exists.
5. Time awareness	:	punctuality; brevity; good use of time.

What Some Buyers Say

As in all marketing and sales matters, the customer should always have the last word. Let this book be no exception to this rule. Some impromptu comments from TACK's last survey were:

> 'I have three key questions about salespeople:
>
> - Do they care about my objectives?
> - Do they understand my priorities and needs?
> - Are they offering me a solution which suits me best?'

> 'I dislike salespeople with poor listening skills, poor knowledge of my systems and lack of commitment to deadlines.'

> 'The main points which concern me are:
> - their manner
> - ttheir ability to listen
> - that they don't waste time
> - that they get to the point
> - and that they answer my questions.'

'I do find it bad when I, as a customer, have to chase up quotes, etc.'

'The level of professionalism in salespeople is getting much better.'

CONCLUSION

The final comment above is good to hear for all of us who care about making the sales profession just that – a profession. Above all else, we must remember always to see things from the customer's point of view and talk in the following terms:

mainly of YOU	–	the customer
secondly of WE	–	the customer and supplier
and finally of I	–	the salesperson.

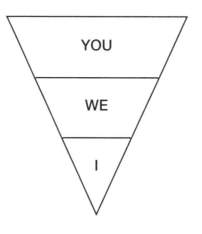

Index